The American West. Visions and Revisions

This is a succinct survey of the numerous contributions to the
history of the American west. In the past twenty-five years historians
have created a 'New Western History', which has aimed to rewrite
the 'Old Western History' built around the famous Turner thesis on
the significance of the American Frontier. Focusing on five main
themes, this study examines and discusses the dynamics and progress of recent scholarship. Consideration is given to issues of land
use, the environment, race, ethnicity, gender, business and the
development of communities. Synthesising prolific research the
book offers a clear and up-to-date review for all students of
American history. A full bibliography is provided for more extended
study.

MARGARET WALSH is Professor of American Economic and Social
History in the School of American and Canadian Studies at the
University of Nottingham. She is author and editor of several books
and many articles on economic and social history, most recently,
Making Connections: The Long Distance Bus Industry in the USA
(2000).

D0162334

New Studies in Economic and Social History

Edited for the Economic History Society by
Maurice Kirby
Lancaster University

This series, specially commissioned by the Economic History Society, provides a guide to the current interpretations of the key themes of economic and social history in which advances have recently been made or in which there has been significant debate.

In recent times economic and social history has been one of the most flourishing areas of historical study. This has mirrored the increasing relevance of the economic and social sciences both in a student's choice of career and in forming a society at large more aware of the importance of these issues in their everyday lives. Moreover, specialist interests in business, agricultural and welfare history, for example, have themselves burgeoned and there has been an increased interest in the economic development of the wider world. Stimulating as these scholarly developments have been for the specialist, the rapid advance of the subject and the quantity of new publications make it difficult for the reader to gain an overview of particular topics, let alone the whole field.

New Studies in Economic and Social History is intended for students and their teachers. It is designed to introduce them to fresh topics and to enable them to keep abreast of recent writing and debates. All the books in the series are written by a recognised authority in the subject, and the arguments and issues are set out in a critical but unpartisan fashion. The aim of the series is to survey the current state of scholarship, rather than to provide a set of pre-packaged conclusions.

The series has been edited since its inception in 1986 by Professors M. W. Flinn, T. C. Smount, L. A. Clarkson and Michael Sanderson, and is currently edited by Professor Maurice Kirby. From 1968 it was published by Macmillan as Studies in Economic History, and after 1974 as Studies in Economic and Social History. From 1995 New Studies in Economic and Social History is being published on behalf of the Economic History Society by Cambridge University Press. This new series includes some of the titles previously published by Macmillan as well as new titles, and reflects the ongoing development throughout the world of this rich seam of history.

For a full list of titles in print, please see the end of the book.

The American West.
Visions and Revisions

Margaret Walsh

CAMBRIDGE
UNIVERSITY PRESS

PUBLISHED BY THE PRESS SYNDICATE OF THE UNIVERSITY OF CAMBRIDGE
The Pitt Building, Trumpington Street, Cambridge CB2 1RP, United
Kingdom

CAMBRIDGE UNIVERSITY PRESS
The Edinburgh Building, Cambridge, CB2 2RU, UK
40 West 20th Street, New York, NY 10011-4211, USA
477 Williamstown Road, Port Melbourne, VIC 3207, Australia
Ruiz de Alarcón 13, 28014 Madrid, Spain
Dock House, The Waterfront, Cape Town 8001, South Africa
http://www.cambridge.org

© Cambridge University Press 2005

First published 2005

Printed in the United Kingdom at the University Press, Cambridge

Typeset in 10/12.5pt Plantin   [PND]

A catalogue record for this book is available from the British Library

Library of Congress Cataloguing in Publication data

Walsh, Margaret, 1942–
    The American West / Margaret Walsh.
        p.   cm. – (New studies in economic and social history;v. 50)
    Includes bibliographical references and index.
    ISBN 0 521 59333 6 (hardback) – ISBN 0 521 59671 8 (paperback)
    1. West (US) – History.   2. West (US) – Economic
    conditions.   3. West (US) – Social conditions.   I. Title.   II. New
    studies in economic and social history; 50.
F591. W258   2004
978 – DC22
                                                    2004051855

Contents

Maps

Tables

Acknowledgements

It is impossible for a British historian to undertake research and writing on American history without financial assistance. I am very grateful to the British Academy who awarded me their fellowship to the Huntington Library in 1996. The Huntington provides the resources and companionship of what ranks as an 'El Dorado' to a scholar of American Western History. I am also very grateful to the Institute for Advanced Study at Indiana University which welcomed me as a Visiting Scholar in the autumn of 2002 and thereby facilitated my use of Western materials at the university's substantial holdings. My own School of American and Canadian Studies and the University of Nottingham financially supported this visit to Bloomington.

I also wish to acknowledge the ideas generated and the audiences provided by both undergraduate students and MA students at the University of Nottingham. Chris Wrigley read and wisely commented on the earlier versions of this manuscript and provided support and encouragement throughout its gestation. I alone am responsible for any errors in the text.

1

The frontier and the west: realities, myths and the historians

There are many American wests. Generations of academics, especially the historians, have argued about what the west is and where it is, none more vehemently than in recent years. Generations of 'others', a collective name which is currently very popular among academics and which here denotes artists, authors or writers, film makers and entertainers have also looked at the west with diverse eyes. Frequently these others have been labelled as distillers of culture usually of the popular variety. At times the historians and the others have bumped into each other and have used each other's materials and ideas, more so of late as popular culture has become a subject for academic inquiry. But for the most part the two streams remain apart, frequently decrying each other's western visions because the academic is based on 'facts' while the popular relies on fictions and creates myths. Though the modern academic turn to cultural interpretations has led to more efforts to interchange respective visions, there remain possibly as many wests as there are interpreters.

Turner and the Frontier thesis

The debate about the nature, extent and progress of the American west has its academic roots in the late nineteenth century. Though some commentators point to the future president Theodore Roosevelt's epic-style four volumes, *The Winning of the West* published between 1885 and 1894, as a moulder of historical views, most historians consider that the Wisconsin historian, Frederick Jackson Turner, penned the original professional vision in 1893.

He certainly penned the most famous vision in his essay, 'The Significance of the Frontier in American History', where he talked about the existence of an area of free land and its continuous recession as American settlers moved west. The frontier as a place with a population density of under two persons per square mile explained American development. The abundance of available and free or cheap land provided the material foundation which enabled millions of people to build the United States into the wealthy and democratic nation that was visible at the turn of the twentieth century.

How did this 'frontier process' happen? Starting in the seventeenth century settlers pushed inland from the Atlantic coast to utilise 'free land', moving in a series of evolutionary stages progressing from simple to complex. The record of this social evolution

> begins with the Indian and the hunter...it goes on to tell of...the trader...the pastoral stage in ranch life, the exploitation of the soil by the raising of unrotated crops...in sparsely settled communities; the intensive culture of the denser farm settlement; and finally the manufacturing organisation with city and factory system.   (Turner, 1893)

Such a process of civilisation proceeded from the Cumberland Gap in Maryland to South Pass in the Rocky Mountains. Turner used the *Statistical Atlas*, based on the United States Census of 1890, to document this process and to show how it had spread across the continent and how, in his opinion, it was coming to a close. He thus created a national historical interpretation. At some point then in the American past the whole nation was part of the west.

In addition to being a means of evolutionary growth and geographical settlement Turner's frontier was also the source of American character. It was a major social force. As settlers moved west across the continent their confrontation with the savage Indians and the wilderness forced them to abandon their traditional customs and practices and to become new persons, the Americans. This repetitive engagement with western frontiers gave Americans

> that coarseness and strength combined with acuteness and inquisitiveness; that practical turn of mind, quick to find expedients; that masterful grasp of material things, lacking in the artistic, but powerful to effect great ends; that restless nervous energy, that dominant individualism and withal that buoyance and exuberance which comes with freedom...   (Turner, 1893)

Such frontier traits became American traits because the frontier experience was transmitted both geographically through space and historically through time. The pioneers also created and bequeathed democracy in a similar way because their struggle with the primitive environment encouraged active participation in public affairs. Regarding themselves as the equals of anyone, they spread democratic ideas to all parts of the nation.

Early responses to the thesis

Turner's thesis was the product of years of hard work and was an amalgam of many interdisciplinary ideas. Yet when he presented his paper orally in 1893 and when he sent copies shortly thereafter to other historians and to newspaper and magazine editors, he received perfunctory, unenthusiastic and even discouraging responses. This was not surprising. His basic propositions questioned orthodox institutional and political history and his general and poetic style failed to satisfy the rigorous and analytical methods of social scientists. He must have been a disappointed scholar. Undeterred, he continued to promote his western ideas. He disseminated them in his teaching – and he had many postgraduate students who went on to academic careers. He wrote in popular journals. He gave many public talks and he worked his way up the professional historical association to become a notable figure. By the early twentieth century his thesis was widely recognised in the academic world. Many western history courses were taught in universities and there was a Turnerian school of history (Billington, R. A., 1973; Walsh, 1992; Bogue, 1998).

The thesis fitted the optimistic mood of the United States at the turn of the century. Domestically Turnerian ideas often distilled by others in popular magazines, newspapers and public lectures, fitted both with the optimistic reforming ethos of Progressivism and a growing sense of national pride. Externally the nation was now recognised as a world power because of its economic prowess and it was beginning to look overseas to extend its imperial influence. There was nothing that the Americans could not achieve. They were unique or exceptional and this exceptionalism came from their own internal strength, endowed by the frontier settlement process (Wrobel, 1993, pp. viii–ix).

This type of positive and triumphant frontierism did not remain unchallenged. A reaction set in during the 1930s and early 1940s. Turner's vision revelled in the abundance of American resources. The 1930s, however, was a decade of pessimism and lack of opportunity, known as 'The Great Depression'. The decade saw rates of 25 per cent unemployment in its early years and unemployment never fell below 14 per cent despite massive government spending. A nation unable to overcome serious economic difficulties was a far cry from the robust and optimistic country portrayed by Turner. So he became unfashionable for contemporary reasons. He was also criticised for intellectual reasons. His thesis was grounded in a rural past or perhaps, more accurately, in an underdeveloped or developing economy. Clearly a nation which had become the world's leading industrial economy and was officially recognised as urban in 1920 had other explanations of its past. Furthermore as the world's leading modern immigrant society, the contributions of a medley of peoples offered insights into the distinctive nature of the American past. So there were alternative interpretations of the American past, which offered as, if not more, plausible explanations than the frontier. What is more, a detailed analysis of the thesis revealed verbal inconsistencies, for example, in the use of the term 'frontier', a tendency to generalise and internal contradictions. It also displayed elements of provincialism because the Mountain West, the South West and Far West were either ignored or at best marginalised (Billington, R. A., 1973; Jacobs, 1994; Bogue, 1998).

Old Western History

Though Turner's western vision lost its pre-eminence among historians looking for explanations of the American past, it did not die. The thesis was resurrected or revised for another generation, not only of Americans, but also of industrial westernised societies. Following the Second World War the Americans again enjoyed another period of confidence, optimism and material wealth. They had triumphed during the war and their economy had not only recovered, but had surged to high levels of productivity. Once again exceptionalism became the flavour of the day. This time an historian with better professional credentials than Turner carried the frontier experience to both the academic world and the American people. Ray Allen Billington produced the textbook that Turner never wrote. *Westward Expansion*, first published in 1949, was a massive tome which grew larger with each edition until its latest abridged version in 2001 (Billington, R. A., 1949). This volume literally saw hundreds of thousands of readers and educated many hundreds of academics. Billington did not stop here. He was a prolific researcher and writer, producing at least fifteen 'western' books and/or pamphlets as well as numerous articles, which all helped to reinstate Turner's reputation in the historical profession. Furthermore, Billington was an inspiring lecturer, teaching thousands of students and through his postgraduate students, thousands more of what he called 'his intellectual grandchildren'. He gave many public lectures, popularising his interpretations and, like Turner, he advanced up the profession not only to national, but also to international standing (Ridge, 1987; Oglesby, 1988; Limerick, 1991).

The evidence he and his supporters gathered provided more detailed information about western history by examining themes and testing ideas set within the frontier framework. Books with frontier in their title flourished. Billington stimulated some of this interest by founding the *Histories of the American Frontier Series* in 1961. This series originally aimed to examine regional and topical histories of the frontier experience as in Rodman W. Paul's *The Mining Frontier of the Far West, 1848–1880* (1963) or Oscar Winther's *The Transportation Frontier. Trans-Mississippi West, 1865–1890* (1965). It was subsequently extended to include areas and themes like the Mexican Borderlands and Latin America and peoples like Native Americans and women. The post-war wave of social scientists eager to test theory and increasingly equipped with computers capable of facilitating quantitative analysis also found in Turner's thesis a series of questions and ideas that they could analyse (Elkins and McKitrick, 1954; Curti, 1959; Mann, 1982). Furthermore, 'Turnerianism' was taken overseas. Scholars talked about comparative frontiers when examining settlements in grassland nations or in areas which were developed in the same timeframe as the American west (Sharp, 1955a; Hennessey, 1978; Lamar and Thompson, 1981). By the 1960s frontier had become a 'buzz' word and had moved more firmly into the rhetoric of American history.

It had also moved into popular language. Unlike Europe where frontier means a barrier or a political boundary, frontier in the United States became synonymous with opportunity and the potential to achieve anything. President John F. Kennedy spoke of the frontiers of space, referring to the space race of the 1960s. The science fiction television series *Star Trek* regularly introduced itself by sending spacecraft to new frontiers where no one else had gone before. Indeed the nation could conquer any frontier and frontier imagery became both potent and persuasive. The growth of area studies, like American Studies in the 1960s and 1970s, in part funded by American money overseas, stimulated a multidisciplinary or an interdisciplinary approach to the west and consolidated the all-encompassing frontier dynamic. Historians were introduced to new ideas and they were encouraged to use the tools and techniques of literary and cultural analysis. Academic interest in the west was lively even though it was cast in the framework established by Turner some sixty–seventy years earlier.

Modern revisionism

But this post-war vision of the American west would not remain vibrant for long in the academic world. Already in the 1970s western historians were becoming anxious and were talking about the lethargy of their subject. There were more than enough micro-studies exploring aspects of Turner's thesis. Historians and social scientists were merely adding more examples, consolidating the status quo and producing nothing new and exciting. Even worse, western history as a subject seemed to be losing its attraction as other types of history, for example, urban, economic, political and immigrant, flourished in their 'revisioned' mode as 'New Histories'. This state of unease, however, proved short-lived. A cluster of historians who eventually became known as the New Western Historians were already doing research for articles and books which would shake up any feelings of complacency and stir up a mass, and at times, an acrimonious response. Furthermore, diverse groups of historians like women's, ecological or ethnohistorians, who based their work in the American west, but who drew their ideas from other theoretical and methodological areas, were also creating fresh perspectives.

Of these academics the New Western Historians created most controversy. In setting out their agendas they needed first to encounter and to dismiss Frederick Jackson Turner. Unlike their counterparts in the 1930s they did not want to bury Turner, either in his original format or in the revised shape in which he had made a comeback in the post-war years. As modern revisionists they aimed to cremate him and scatter his ashes to the winds. Turner's vision, or more accurately that of Billington and his followers, now called Old Western Historians, was deemed to be far too discriminatory and triumphalist for post-modern society. Liberal social awareness had created an environment in which all Americans, whether they were racial or ethnic minorities or women, were to be fully recognised. Ecological studies increasingly pointed to the scarcity of resources and past wasteful patterns of exploitation, while political insecurity in the wake of the Vietnam War had shaken Americans' confidence in their world superiority and their imperial ventures (Worster, 1985; White, 1991). In the 1980s and 1990s the more complex vision of New Western History talked about legacies of conquest (Limerick, 1987). The dark side of western history was not only revealed, but became its dominant face.

Set within specific geographical boundaries, sometimes of the Trans-Mississippi West, but more often of the Trans-Missouri West and the Pacific coast, though occasionally including Hawaii and Alaska (Nugent, 1992), the New West, as a region, became a neo-colonial area. Whether in the seventeenth or the twentieth centuries, it was controlled by outsiders. The French, Spanish, British and Russians all used the area for their mercantile ambitions. The Americans, once they gained their independence, ensured that the west would remain subordinate either because of a lengthy territorial system which denied the area early self-determination or through federal control over large portions of western natural resources. Even public spending on the defence industry and conservation kept the west subservient. Gone was the freedom and individualism of Turner's frontier. In the New Western History opportunities were few and far between. Greedy capitalists exploited such western labourers as miners and loggers by paying poor wages. The mineral and lumbering wealth was taken out of the region leaving massive debris. Aridity in much of the region necessitated outside control over natural resources. Cities and towns suffered in a boom and slump style development and many farmers were disillusioned as their chances of success were destroyed by the weather or by such middlemen as railroad companies, bankers and landlords. There were, as Patricia Limerick suggested, more uncertain enterprises than triumphant individualists (Limerick, 1987).

The New Western Historians not only established the failures and disappointments of a colonised and exploited west with a continuous past which stretched from prehistoric times to the present; they also helped change its demographic face. Turner's western vision was white and masculine. Though Old Western Historians did include Native Americans and some ethnic minorities in their narratives, they often treated them as the 'others' or as different from, and marginal to, the superior white man. And they failed to recognise women. New Western Historians were able to draw on earlier research in ethnohistory and women's history to demonstrate an ethnically mixed if not a burgeoning multicultural society.

Ethnohistory, concerned with aboriginal pasts, had already drawn on the findings and methods of social anthropology, ethnology, archaeology and oral traditions to gain knowledge of Native American communities both pre- and post-1492 when Columbus reached the Americas (Axtell, 1997). Native peoples were increasingly being understood in the context of their own languages, customs and ways of life (Jacobs, 1973; Edmunds, 1995, pp. 723–6). Furthermore, their meeting with Turner's westward moving pioneers, now called imperial conquerors, was interpreted in the light of white greed, stupidity and inefficiency as well as native problems such as intertribal warfare. United States' Indian policy was a contested academic terrain in which federal authority was condemned, questioned or at least debated rather than being accepted at face value (Hagan, 1997; Fixico, 1997a; Deloria, 2002). Such findings well suited the tenor of New Western History approaches.

Women's historians initially were concerned to make women visible as real people and to banish traditional female images portrayed in long-suffering, dauntless or deviant stereotypes. They both put white females into Turner's westward-moving process and they challenged that process by recognising the importance of these women's domestic role in settling the west. Without the female contributions to the home and the community, whether rural or urban, there would have been no settlement and growth.

The feminine role of housewife, mother, co-farmworker, teacher, hotel manager, reformer or prostitute may be less romantic or adventurous than the heroic masculinity portrayed by trappers, explorers, cowboys or the military, but it was no less fundamental (Myres, 1982; Riley, 1988; Walsh, 1995; Jeffrey, 1998). So too was the later acknowledgement of ethnic and racial minorities by women's historians. Inclusive women's western history, more often called multicultural women's history, has aimed to examine all women rather than only Euro-American women as active decision-making people. As yet it has been limited to examining experiences within specific groups, looking at power relationships and cultural values. Much work still remains to be done before all women can be fully integrated into, or can transform, the history of the American west (Jameson and Armitage, 1997).

Part of the newer, ethnically aware transformation of western history included minority men as well as women even though much more research again needs to be undertaken. The west was home to Asian-Americans, Mexican-Americans and African-Americans and to religious minorities. Though these groups, either singly or together, were not numerically dominant, their place in western society had started to be recognised and analysed. Asian Americans may have remained culturally isolated but their labour in the mines, building railroads and providing household services was an essential part of economic growth. Their contributions, however, were made as a segregated group and their lives were severely marked by social and legal discrimination. Mexican Americans also suffered from discrimination. Their prior settlement in the area rarely gave them access to better conditions, as most had been peon labourers on the land. Even the landed elite often found that they could not resist the pressures and the authority of white American newcomers. African-Americans moving from the American south, primarily as free persons after the Civil War may have suffered less discrimination and harassment, but they still faced racial prejudice as workers, as voters and in social settings. Mormons, living in Utah, were also disliked or barely tolerated as their religion set them aside from the mainstream. Given such tensions, discussions of western history framed in a multicultural society have offered a much more negative outlook than earlier interpretations (Limerick, 1987, pp. 222–92; Taylor, 1998; De Leon, 2002). Recognition of diversity has brought losers as well as winners, but understanding the full demographic experience suggests a greater appreciation of the complexity of the past.

The New Western Historians

Collectively the revisionists revitalised the general interest in western history, but of these, the New Western Historians, often considered the main protagonists, stimulated a long and strident academic debate. Though their interpretations were not always new, they proclaimed them with a vigour that called for a response. Both Old Western Historians and not so old historians replied, frequently in kind without couching their comments in polite academic language. *Rivers of Empire* (1985), a very important volume on the western environment was labelled 'deeply flawed – arrogant, distorted and moralistic' (Pisani, 1988, p. 319). The major textbook, *It's Your Misfortune and None of My Own* (1991) was deemed to be more concerned with minorities than with everyone and was re-titled 'A Victim's History of the American West'. *Legacy of Conquest* (1987), probably the most influential volume of the New Western History was perceived to pay too much attention to continuity at the expense of significant changes, thereby sacrificing historical balance for journalistic appeal (Symposium, 1993; Thompson, 1994; Nash, G. D., 1994). *Nature's Metropolis* (1991) and *Under an Open Sky* (1992) escaped much of the name-calling, probably because William Cronon has not easily been typecast as a New Western Historian. The 'cheerleaders' of this brand of modern revisionism should perhaps have been called the 'gang of three' rather than the 'gang of four'.

The naming of the leading protagonists as a gang, thereby implying a bunch of hooligans or criminals, was a media stunt. The 1989 symposium, 'Trails: Toward a New Western History' led to a statement by its convenor Patricia Limerick, entitled 'What on Earth is the New Western History? '(Limerick *et al.*, 1991, pp. 85–7). Several participants also referred to the New Western History. Journalists then decided that a new academic movement was afoot and publicised this approach in a range of newspapers and magazines (Limerick *et al.* 1991, pp. 59–61; Wrobel, 1996b). For example, *The Milwaukee Journal* of 11 October 1989 proclaimed that

a corps of academic Young Turks has mounted a full scale war against one of the most influential intellectual concepts in American history: Frederick Jackson Turner's famous 'frontier thesis'.
The scholars promoting what they call the "new Western history" are teaching... that Turner's powerful idea... is racist, sexist, wrong, irrelevant – or all of the above.

The media, treasuring the romanticism and optimism of frontierism was not only telling their public what the historians were 'up to', but was also fuelling an adversarial atmosphere in which academics were expected to do battle.

Much of this academic revisioning did not meet with popular approval. There were cries of outrage as the New Western Historians brought dirt, exploitation, class warfare and racism to general attention. As the new mood of academic interpretation swept the art world too, there were vociferous protests to Congress when exhibits displayed the grey, if not black side of the westward experience. 'The West as America: Reinterpreting Images of the Frontier, 1820–1920', held at the Smithsonian Institution in Washington DC from March to July 1991 and 'Discovered Lands, Invented Pasts: Transforming Visions of the American West', displayed at various institutions from mid-1992 to mid-1993, brought howls of protests and complaints about political correctness. In response the New Western Historians claimed numerous supporters among westerners, in the general reading public and in academia. But many more Americans, both in the west as a region and in the nation at large, had been brought up on a diet that included western heroes, an ethic of individualistic success and a philosophy of 'can do' (Wrobel, 1996b).

This diet, however misguided and myopic, had a long pedigree. Myths and misconceptions of what the west was and what some Americans, often easterners, wanted the west to be, was contemporary with the settlement of newly acquired lands. For example, the legend of Davy Crockett, frontiersman, congressman from Tennessee and hero of the Alamo, emerged from comic almanacs that originated in 1835 and were published through to 1856. Crockett was also a character in the dime novels or romantic pulp fiction published initially in the 1840s, but which littered the country by the ton load after the Civil War. He along with other real westerners, such as Kit Carson, Billy the Kid, Calamity Jane and

William F. Cody, better known as Buffalo Bill, sat alongside fictional creations such as Deadwood Dick, Rattlesnake Ned and the Black Avenger. These novels, together with their romantic illustrations early glamorised western individuals into some kind of fantasy icons (Etulain, 1999, pp.17–19; Hine and Faragher, 2000, pp. 476–7). Here were 'creation stories' in the making.

Contemporary biographies, travelogues, newspaper stories, Wild West shows and art repackaged through cheap lithographs consolidated western myths in the late nineteenth century. They were soon supported and expanded by western fiction and motion pictures, both frequently featuring the heroic figure of the cowboy (Etulain, 1999, pp. 5–25; Hine and Faragher, 2000, pp. 498–508). These two entertainment forms would remain popular for much of the twentieth century helping to confirm what historians William H. and William N. Goetzmann have called *The West of the Imagination* (1986), a dream-like fantasy that provided an escape from daily routine. The post-war packaged Disney versions of the west, with their Davy Crocketts in coonskin caps, Buffalo Bill Wild West shows and Mark Twain riverboat rides, have served to consolidate the romantic myth for millions worldwide.

So ingrained in the popular psyche has such imagery become that it appealed not only as escapism, but also as a genuine source of cultural values and a true portrayal of the historical past. Certainly numerous western myths did become historical sources in their own right, reflecting the values of those who produced them and the issues of their times. William F. Cody, for example, did prospect for gold, was a Pony Express rider, a scout for the army and a buffalo hunter; but his Wild West shows in the late nineteenth and early twentieth centuries tended to exaggerate his life and the lives of his western contemporaries. While the dramas in such shows were fictions or staged history, they became part of the real past by dint of their performance and their very popularity (Etulain, 1999, pp. 5–25). In doing so they contributed to a general perception of western history. The contemporary academic turn to cultural interpretations has brought much greater awareness of this process of filtering perceptions and of recognising social expectations (Hyde, 1996, pp. 157–201). But this intellectual practice has not been communicated widely despite the mass-viewing audiences for western docu-dramas and documentaries in which professional historians participate. It is thus not surprising that there has been both a negative media and a grassroots reaction to the demystifying and prosaic tenor of the New Western History that was concerned to refocus the history of Anglo-American perceptions of the west.

More new visions

While the New Western History has dominated the recent visions of the American west, other contributions examining the extent and nature of the west have made an impact on general awareness and interpretations and to historiographical debates. These views sometimes overlap with, have been subsumed by, or follow from New Western History and have sometimes been called new western history, but they merit discussion in their own right. Of the surveys, William Robbins' Marxist approach in *Colony & Empire. The Capitalist Transformation of the American West* (1994) has been the most provocative. In investigating the impact of capitalism on a west that stretches from the mid-nineteenth century to the late twentieth century and that crosses national boundaries, he echoed the negativism of the New Western Historians in his findings. The west, its resources and its labourers were exploited as part of a continually changing and expansive global market system. Robbins' discussion of the complexity of capitalist networks in the west, the relationships of hinterlands to cities and of external capital to western development placed the area firmly in an economic context that shattered traditional romanticism. However, his overarching framework not only placed him on the margins of mainstream western history, but also of American historians who have rarely been able to assimilate radical, left-wing interpretations.

Regionalists who have challenged the boundaries of the New Western History, or whose central concerns have offered a different approach to and perspective on the west, offer further insights into setting agendas for historical inquiry. Borderlands history has an interpretative past that stretches back to the early twentieth century when Herbert Bolton talked about a northward pushing frontier (Bolton, 1921; Worcester, 1991, pp. 193–213) and established a Boltonian school of interpretation. Primarily focused on the southwestern quadrant of the United States it traditionally emphasised the imperial connections to Spain, the Catholic religion and inter-racial contacts and had an audience primarily within its own regional boundaries. It was, however, also of interest to academics of Latin American or Mexican history as the northern frontier of Spain. Recently these historians have engaged with the debates about whether and how the missions exploited indigenous labour and customs (Sweet, 1995; Jackson, 1998a). Historians interested in the past of the United States have in contrast given more attention to the multicultural history of the southwest. Their insights into places where Hispanic peoples, many of whom were mestizos, struggled for influence and resources with Native Americans, Europeans and with each another, has raised such central concerns as occupation, inter-racial relationships and transformations of the landscape. Such issues have always been important in western his-tory (Weber, 1994, pp. 73–5). They need, however, to be perceived with eyes that look in a different direction from the westward moving Euro-American settlers.

Another sub-regional interpretation or school of western history, which also had a northward-looking focus, originated with Texas historian Walter Prescott Webb in the 1930s. Taking the arid west of the mid-continent as his focus he examined *The Great Plains* (1931) as a social science historian and an ecologist. Contending that environmental conditions influenced human behaviour, he pointed to the dangers as well as the possibilities of pushing settlement into arid lands. Though he welcomed the answers that technology could provide to overcome the problems of utilising nature for capi-talist endeavours, he also recognised potential negative consequences. The vicious dust storms of the 1930s, collectively known as the Dust Bowl, brought home to Americans the message of ecological disaster. And Webb's later writings warned more directly about incorrect land use (West, 1991, pp. 167–91).

This environmental concern about the mid-continent, which ear-lier explorers and scientists had called 'The Great American Desert', came back into modern historical fruition in the work of one of the New Western Historians, Donald Worster. His first book, *Dust Bowl* (1979) arraigned the federal government for its disastrous policies that encouraged over-use of a landscape not naturally given to intensive farming. This volume appeared prior to New Western History. But Worster's second volume, *Rivers of*

Empire (1985) soon placed him in that revisionist mode as he labelled the arid area a hydraulic region dependent on an imperial elite that had created complex irrigation systems to serve the needs of increasing populations. Western people, especially after the Second World War, were not living in harmony with nature. Worster continued to pound the environmental beat into the 1990s with collections of essays and a book on environmental history (Worster, 1992, 1994). He, together with William Cronon and Richard White, gave New Western History a strong environmental cast. Such work built on and strengthened the messages of another group of western historians writing on water in the 1960s and 1970s (Huntley, 1996, pp. 5–11). Had it not been for the popular and academic commotion about New Western History a fully fledged ecological interpretation of the west as a region might have become more prevalent. If such a school had developed and had looked for a 'forefather' then Walter Prescott Webb would have been a strong contender. Certainly Donald Worster recognised the academic debt he owed to Webb, even suggesting in 1987 that 'I know in my bones, if not always through my education, that Webb was right' (Worster, 1992, p. 24).

Another, though as yet embryonic challenge to the regional and geographical boundaries suggested by New Western History, lies in northern borderlands history. Traditionally Canada has not attracted a strong comparative historical approach because the American/Canadian border is less visible than its American/Mexican counterpart in the south. Settled predominantly by European immigrants and controlled by an imperial, white and English-speaking government, with relatively little movement across the border, the north has never become a major threat. Early suggestions of comparative work (Sharp, 1955a, 1955b) were rarely pursued. Of late, however, historians have become interested in such comparative work. They consider, for example, similarities in landscape and ecology in the American plains and the Canadian prairies and they analyse comparative attitudes to, and treatments of social arrangements for native peoples and law and order (McLaren *et al.*, 1992; Nichols, 1998; Higham, 2000; Binnema *et al.*, 2001; LaDow, 2001). Yet further west on the Pacific coast the contention that British Columbia is quite distinct from the prairie provinces (Barman, 1991) has again raised the debate about whether the Pacific coast region as a whole is different to the plains and the mountain regions. Perhaps a more natural harmony would emerge from studying the northwest as an area that ignored political boundaries (Robbins, 2001). Fruitful comparative analysis of similarities and differences that cross borders offers diverse insights into what has made the American west distinct and what is perceived to be important in these distinctions.

So too does the recognition of an early west that flourished in the trans-Appalachian country. The Midwest, however defined (Cayton and Gray, 2001, pp. 1–26), shared some of the same problems and characteristics of the western region identified in New Western History as it developed and its history can be linked quite clearly in terms of settlement patterns. It is true that the linkage became weaker in the twentieth century (Madison, 1997, p. 46), but the common threads so useful to assessing regionalism have been force-fully cut in the recent ascendancy of New Western History with its rejection of the Turnerian package. Yet research on early western settlements involving intercultural contacts between natives and incomers and the exploitation of resources like furs and minerals have provided valuable insights into issues that western historians consider vital (White, 1991; Cayton and Tuete, 1998; Murphy, L.E. 2000; Sleeper-Smith, 2001). The retention of 'frontier' in the title of some of this work, even though the focus is contested spaces or zones, as well as its geographical location has impeded profitable connections between diverse western historians who seek to under-stand the complex layering of neighbouring areas. There is much to be learned from developing a fluidity that can cross the 'mental territories' that have constructed academic and emotional bound-aries round the American west.

The recognition of and engagement with porous regional bound-aries and flexible western identities has raised interesting questions. When it became apparent that there was no consensus among wes-terners about the extent and nature of their region (Nugent, 1992), some historians tried to elucidate a definable academic position. David Emmons, for example, identified one large constructed region emerging in the 1840s and consolidating after the Civil War. Such a west acknowledged a region that was as easily recognisable as was the other major American region, the south. But this west still con-tained sub-regions. Historians commenting on this attempt to create a consensus found major difficulties in agreeing to the region as a whole, let alone to the smaller units that they considered could be identified as geographical or perhaps bio-environmental, cultural, economic, political or even imagined. It seems that whenever historians discussed the west on their own terms there was a set of shifting parameters (Emmons, 1994; Roundtable, 1994, 2000).

Turner's vision re-framed

Even with the abundance of new western visions there remained historians who wished to retain some of Frederick Jackson Turner's ideas in establishing a viable 'greater west'. They too faced dissent and have not been effective in establishing the parameters of western history. William Cronon has perhaps been the leading historian to retain Turnerian links. Though identified by many as a New Western Historian he never formally nailed his colours to that mast. He always maintained that Turner left a legacy that was worth salvaging. Certainly the thesis as a whole was seriously flawed. But Turner's concept of a west that shifted over time while still relating to the wider history of the nation, that recognised the interaction of people with landscapes and that put people in the centre was worth salvaging (Cronon, 1987, p. 171; Roundtable, 2000, pp. 477–8). There was a great west story in which 'the transition from frontier to region was a process of creating new, more stable geographic identities in the midst of landscapes that people chose to perceive as homes' (Cronon, 1992, p. 3). A greater west also functioned for Stephen Aron for whom the mingling of natives and newcomers in cultural and economic exchanges in the trans-Appalachian west was also part of the 'conquest, colonization and capitalist consolidation of the continent' (Aron, 1994, p. 127). Here indigenous communities were incorporated into imperial or perhaps global capitalist systems in a process that created new local or western identities. Frontier may be a word with a past that has become tainted over the years, but it did encompass change over time and through space and was inclusive (Klein, K. L. 1996, pp. 208–15; Adelman and Aron, 1999; pp. 814–16).

There are, historiographically, New Western Historians, Old Western Historians, new and old versions of each and many

in-between. (Wrobel, 1996; Wunder, 1994, 1998). The vision of the
American west presented here, as other visions, is personal because
my cultural perspectives, geographical location and research experience and training mould its framework. Yet at the same time it is a
collective vision because its contents have been selected from what
is now a vast treasure-trove of historiographical and historical
resources. It is not always a west that explores from east to west,
but it does encompass a large geographical area that has in the
American past been called western. It works within a capitalist
framework, which involves use and misuse of resources, an individualistic ethos, which puts a premium on self-worth, a political
value-system capable of sufficient flexibility to be called democratic
and colonial simultaneously and a cultural heritage which has popular as well as academic dimensions.

The west is thus a study of a developing economy in the expansionist era of the primarily nineteenth-century world. That this
economy was part of an independent nation rather than being
a European colony, that the newly formed nation had declared itself
democratic and that it claimed abundant natural resources and
recognised an indigenous population creates numerous tensions
and at times apparent contradictions in understanding its past.
Furthermore, the contrasts between, and its connections with, the
eastern part of the nation have defied easy analysis. While native
peoples were being finally subdued at the Battle of Wounded Knee
in 1890, the United States was announcing its industrial prowess to
the world at large. The census of that year may well not proclaim the
end of the Turnerian frontier of settling empty lands, but it does
demonstrate the growth of the country from a struggling nation to
a leading power. The American west, its context and its connections,
remains exciting, but also perplexing and challenging to interpret.

2
Land and landscapes: ownership and occupation

Land has always been abundant in the United States regardless of who perceives this resource. For the original inhabitants, whether as hunting, gathering, fishing, trading or agrarian communities, it was possible to occupy, survive and thrive for many years and there were still hundreds of thousands of acres not used. For European immigrants, land seemed plentiful, especially when compared to its scarcity in their original homelands. Furthermore, it was fertile land and once used for intensive farming it could yield an improved standard of living. It was also frequently beautiful as landscape and as such attracted the attention of artists and environmentalists, who wanted to conserve it as a natural wilderness for their and future generations. The ownership and occupation of western land was both desired and then contested by many peoples.

Native peoples on the land

No historian fully appreciates or can identify the varieties of landscapes that existed when Native Americans first inhabited the North American continent some 12,000 years ago. Anthropologists, geographers, ethnographers, biologists and some historians have attempted to reconstruct original sites and patterns of vegetation, using scientific techniques, material culture evidence, oral traditions and more conventional historical methodology. But virgin territory or even habitat transformation remains a disputed subject. There are many estimates and suggestions of what was or might have been and concerns with ecology, environment and land use has been high on the agendas of western historians. But the techniques for recovering the forms of original landscapes are essentially unstable (White, 1997, pp. 87–100). What is clearer is that communities of native peoples changed the environment to suit their purposes and thus any claim that they lived in harmony with nature is dubious. Native groups may not have utilised the land so intensively or made as many alterations as did later Euro-Americans and Americans using machine technology, but they were by no means pioneer environmentalists living in an unspoiled Eden (Warren, 2002, pp. 287–9).

The North American continent, prior to contact with European invaders or newcomers in 1492 was thus a landscape marked by many Indian usages. There were possibly as many local adjustments as there were native communities; but climate, vegetation types, other animal and mineral resources had also influenced Indian activities over the course of millennia. Though any suggestions of patterns or events must be received with a degree of caution it seems that diverse disciplinary research offers some general observations about early land use and change. Such statements are framed by estimates of major climatic changes. These shaped the landscape and facilitated the transition from nomadic migrations, focused on hunting large mammals in the late glacial period, to more mixed cultures or economies that included hunting smaller animals, gathering, fishing and some agrarian activities in post-glacial years. Subsequently some native groups competed with each other for occupation of lands, which led to migrations and further adaptations. Others survived in relative harmony and traded peaceably or obtained desired goods through raiding periodically. Native groups made many adjustments to the land when gathering and raising food and they used resources for housing and settlements. Furthermore, they expressed their cultural values with goods fashioned from nature, whether wooden artefacts, tools, baskets or clothing. Diverse native peoples had often migrated and adapted nature to their needs long before European expansion overseas brought them into contact with Old World imperialists. Pre-contact landscape change was commonplace (White, 1983, pp. 147–56; Denevan, 1992, pp. 369–85; West, 1998, pp. 17–58).

Native and European contact

The basic idea that native peoples domesticated land, even though the ensuing landscape might look like wilderness to Europeans, is essential to disengaging from the traditional Euro-American idea that land was unoccupied and was virgin territory to be seized (Warren, 2002, p. 289). Furthermore, once native groups engaged in contact with incoming Europeans, yet more terrain was transformed. Whether through the use and spread of European animals and crops or through the desire for manufactured goods, some of which could accelerate depletion, post-contact regimes of hunting, harvesting and cultivating continued to remake the American west. Early European accounts and much later historical interpretations tell directly and indirectly of adjustments made by both natives and newcomers to accommodate diverse institutional agencies, cultural customs and intercontinental trade patterns (Jennings, 1993, pp. 135–305).

In the western Great Lakes, known to the French as *pays d'en haut*, greater pressure was placed on beaver resources when the lands were terrorised by the westward-moving Iroquois hunters in a fur trade war. This landscape of war stimulated relocation of native settlements adjacent to river junctions and portages (White, 1991; Sleeper-Smith, 2001, pp. 11–22). In the central plains the appearance of the horse following the arrival of the Spanish enabled Indians to work more efficiently. Mounted hunters could search more widely for game and could kill more often; they could also travel more extensively in search of plants and water. Furthermore, horses grazed on the short grasses of the high plains. Their role in changing the environment was potentially large (West, 1998, pp. 49–54; Warren, 2002, pp. 294–6). On the Pacific Northwest coast, native communities who traded with exploring parties of several nations acquired metal knives and axes which enabled them to carve and saw more quickly and efficiently. However, their resulting cultural artefacts were dependent on a higher usage of timber resources (Iverson, 1994, pp. 21–8). At many points too, the impact of new diseases like smallpox, malaria, measles, typhoid and diphtheria, some venereal and alcohol related diseases that affected many native communities, caused widespread population reduction (Stiffarm, 1992, pp. 23–54; Thornton, 2002, pp. 70–73). Lands were not tilled, forests replenished themselves and animals restocked. Foreign arrivals thus had an impact on the natural habitat, which historians have now recognised and documented more thoroughly thanks to their use of social science findings and debates and the spiralling growth of the field of ethnohistory (Axtell, 1997, pp. 11–27).

Euro-American land claims

Foreign arrivals also established different patterns of land ownership. Early European expansion across the Atlantic Ocean looked to 'empires of trade' (Gitlin, 1994) because the imperialists understood their mercantile dominance in terms of commodities which could be bartered with their Old World rivals. The Spanish sought a route to the spice trade of the Far East and, in the process, hoped to find precious minerals. The French were happy to locate fish and furs. The Russians also traded for fish and furs on the Pacific while the English eventually looked to tobacco, fish, indigo and sugar. Such commerce could be better secured by permanent settlement than by temporary trading posts and so land needed to be claimed and colonies planted. The Spanish spread east from the Caribbean islands and north through Mexico reaching Florida in the southeast, moving up the centre through Arizona, New Mexico and Texas and reaching Alta California in their last push in the early eighteenth century. By this time the French had long settled in the centre of the continent spreading along the waterways from the St Lawrence, through the Great Lakes, and down the Mississippi River system to the Gulf ports and up the Missouri River. There were many established French centres in the interior before the Anglo-Americans crossed the Appalachians. The Russians moved more slowly down the Pacific coast from Alaska. The English may have dominated migration inland from the Atlantic coast, but they first had to displace the Swedes and the Dutch. Though they successfully planted colonies in the seventeenth and eighteenth centuries and were able to remove their French rivals from much of the continent, their rule too was temporary. Their colonists rebelled to claim independence, the lands on which they had settled and much more in the name of democracy (Meinig, 1986). Americans subsequently called their drive inland 'manifest destiny', but some historians have considered that domestic imperialism is a more appropriate description of the westward and southward movement (Zevin, 1972, pp. 321–5).

The American expansion across native lands and European colonial holdings was initially slow. The new nation needed to establish its international credentials and to strengthen its economic base before considering geographical growth. However, fearing both Indian and foreign threats in its unsettled backcountry and on its borderlands, the government made early attempts to negotiate with the British in Canada and the Great Lakes area and with the French and Spanish in Louisiana. Troops were also dispatched to prevent clashes between native peoples and American pioneers. President Jefferson, sometimes called the intellectual father of expansionism, looked for an early opportunity to spread out and in 1803 bought Louisiana from France in one of the greatest real estate bargains in history. Dissident Americans who had moved to foreign-held lands, in Florida and Texas, actively sought or were encouraged to seek admission, or what was euphemistically called re-admission, to the United States in 1810 and 1836. The government vigorously engaged in boundary adjustments with Spain in the south in 1819 and negotiated the Canadian boundary with Britain in 1818 to consolidate its early land holdings (Perkins, 1993, pp. 54–169 Meinig, 1993, pp. 3–77).

Continuing to push native peoples inland and onto these newly acquired lands, it soon became apparent that even the extensive scope of a nation that spread to the Rocky Mountains was inadequate to contain westward pushing Euro-Americans. Continental ambitions came to the fore in the 1840s. The lone-star republic of Texas was now admitted to the union in 1845. The Oregon country was re-annexed in 1846 following its joint occupation with Britain and the southwestern quadrant of the country was acquired in 1848 after a short war with Mexico. This process of American expansion was influenced by the direct or indirect threat of force or power. By now the United States could dominate any rivals. Only the small Gadsden Purchase from Mexico in 1853, to ensure the route of a transcontinental railroad, and the larger, but then marginal purchase of Alaska from Russia in 1867 were agreed without restraint. In the space of under a century the United States had demonstrated clearly to the Old World that it was not only independent, but also that it could establish its own brand of imperial land settlement (Table 2:1, Map 2:1).

This process had much more to do with the self-interest of land ownership, rapid population increase, commerce and economic growth than it did with the ideology of spreading democratic ideals. To call the expansion 'manifest destiny', as did the spokespersons of the 1840s, thereby implying a natural, honourable and divinely ordained mission, is difficult if not impossible to accept in a modern and multicultural age. However, academics, influenced by the currents of their times and recognising the peculiar flavour of America's push southwards and westwards, fluctuate between using the terms continentalism, informal colonialism, domestic imperialism or a republican empire (Perkins, 1993; Meinig, 1993).

American land and settlement policies

The land that Britain had handed over to the Americans at the end of the War for Independence (1783) initially belonged to individual ex-colonies, now states. After many internal disputes these states agreed to cede the majority of their western land claims to the federal government. Orderly settlement was essential to the health of the new nation. Two pieces of legislation, the Land Ordinance of 1785 and the Northwest Ordinance of 1787 formed the basis for future settlement policy. The former enacted that Indian title to land should first be cleared and land surveyed before it was sold at an auction to the highest bidder. A minimum price per acre and the size-of-purchase unit was established. The latter laid down a framework of a three-stage political process enabling settlers to move from subordinate territory to full statehood. The Northwest Ordinance also provided for a bill of rights ensuring basic liberties (Gates, 1968; Hurt, 1989). Both capitalism or free market access to land and democratic rule featured in the minds of legislators, but so too did the need for financial reliability after a treasury-depleting war and military security in an era when native peoples and world powers still contested North American occupation and ownership.

The federal government may have laid down settlement policies, but it was flexible enough to adapt them to historical and

Table 2:1 Acquisition of the public domain

Acquisition	Total area[1] (acres)	Public domain (acres)	Cost (dollars)	Cost per area of public domain (in cents)
Area conceded to United States by Great Britain in 1783	495,850,880			
Ceded by seven states[2] to				
United States (1781–1802)	236,825,600	233,415,680	6,200,000	2.66
Louisiana Purchase (1803)	529,911,680	523,466,400	23,213,568	4.43
Red River Basin[3]	29,601,920	29,066,880	–	0.00
Cession from Spain (1819)	46,144,640	43,342,720	6,674,057	15.40
Annexation of Texas[4] (1845)	247,060,480			
Oregon Compromise (1846)	183,386,240	180,644,480	–	0.00
Mexican Cession (1848)	338,680,960	334,479,360	–	4.87
Purchase from Texas (1850)	78,926,720	78,842,880	15,496,448	19.65
Gadsden Purchase (1853)	18,988,800	18,961,920	10,000,000	52.74
Alaska Purchase (1867)	375,296,000	365,481,600	7,200,000	1.97
Total public domain		1,807,681,920	85,079,222	4.71[5]

Source: Based on US Dept of Interior, Bureau of Land Management, Public Land Statistics 1964 (Washington, DC, 1965).
[1] Includes inland water
[2] Georgia Cession involved monetary transaction
[3] Authorities differ on the date of acquisition. Some think that it was part of the Louisiana Purchase; others think that it was acquired from Great Britain
[4] Texas retained control of its own public domain
[5] These figures are estimates, as sources differ on both acreage and costs

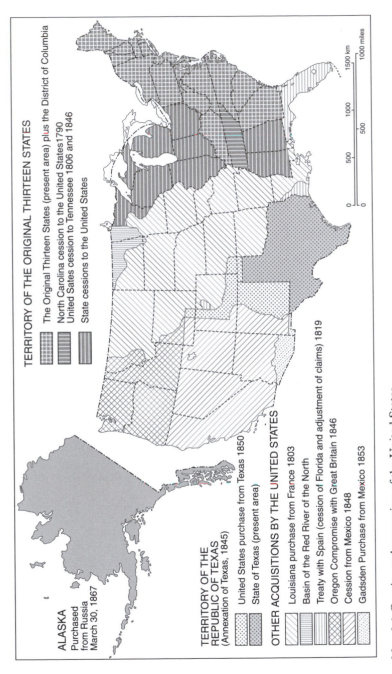

TERRITORY OF THE ORIGINAL THIRTEEN STATES

The Original Thirteen States (present area) plus the District of Columbia

North Carolina cession to the United States 1790
United States cession to Tennessee 1806 and 1846

State cessions to the United States

ALASKA
Purchased
from Russia
March 30, 1867

TERRITORY OF THE
REPUBLIC OF TEXAS
(Annexation of Texas, 1845)

United States purchase from Texas 1850

State of Texas (present area)

OTHER ACQUISITIONS BY THE UNITED STATES

Louisiana purchase from France 1803

Basin of the Red River of the North

Treaty with Spain (cession of Florida and adjustment of claims) 1819

Oregon Compromise with Great Britain 1846

Cession from Mexico 1848

Gadsden Purchase from Mexico 1853

Map 2:1 Continental expansion of the United States.
Source: US Dept. of Interior, Bureau of Land Management, *Public Land Statistics 1964* (Washington, DC, 1965).

geographical circumstances. In the mainstream migration of Euro-American settlement, westward access to land became easier for some incomers and more difficult for others in the nineteenth century. At various times in the early years the government adjusted the size of the minimum land purchase and its price. The Land Ordinance of 1785 set a minimum purchase area of 640 acres, but by 1832 this had been reduced to forty acres. The minimum price of $1.00 per acre in 1785 was subsequently raised to $2.00 in 1796, but was lowered to $1.25 in 1820 where it remained. The government provided credit either in the form of instalment payments, as in 1800, though these were abandoned in 1820, or in the form of kind, as in 1841, by legalising squatting ahead of settlement as a general principle, with the right to purchase a quarter section or 160 acres at the minimum price. It lowered prices on unsold lands in the Graduation Act of 1854, but land was rarely free. The Homestead Act of 1862, which gave 160 acres of land to bona fide settlers, was restricted. The 'free' land was acquired after five years of continuous residence and the payment of registration fees and was not available in certain parts of the west. Certainly some pioneers benefited from this law, but others were disillusioned. Even more resented a free enterprise system that failed to establish a maximum price and a maximum acquisition and thus favoured purchase by large investors, often known as speculators, who then proceeded to resell land at a profit (Table 2:2). They also protested against federal government policy that facilitated the acquisition of substantial blocks of land by rail corporations, lumber companies and large cattle ranchers. There were major inequities in land disposal (Gates, 1968, pp. 121–493; Bogue, 1980).

The flexibility of land disposal policies, often perceived as inconsistencies, has enabled generations of historians to debate official intentions in such language as democratic liberality, economic generosity, incompetent management, inefficient policy or developmental need (Le Duc, 1963; Bogue, 1980, pp. 596–600). Certainly the policies indicated governmental indecision about national objectives and the strength of pressure groups in a democratic society. Perhaps the most fitting description was penned originally in 1936 by the doyen of land historians, Paul Gates, when he talked about 'an incongruous land system' (Gates, 1968, pp. 435–62).

Table 2:2   Disposition of lands in the public domain 1789–1904

Type of disposition	Area (in acres)	Percentage of total
Distributed free[1]	120,227,824	6.64
Grants for construction of all[2] transport networks	127,262,717	7.03
Grants to states and territories (for resale)[3]	155,385,572	8.59
Cash purchase	323,680,138	17.89
Reserved by the government[4]	122,190,579	6.75
Indian reservations	73,045,861	4.04
Unappropriated	841,872,377	46.52
Other[5]	45,874,772	2.54
Total land surface in public domain	**1,809,539,840**	**100.00**

Source: Based on US 58 Cong. 3 Sess. Senate Documents, no 189, *Report* of the Public Lands Commission, 1905.

[1] Includes Indian allotments, but not military bounties
[2] Includes roads, canals, rivers and railroads
[3] Includes school and swamp land acts
[4] Includes federal and state reserves and reclamations
[5] Includes mineral lands, private claims, scrip land, agricultural college lands

Incongruous also applies to federal disposal policy in respect to antecedent settlers, their land occupation and customary ownership patterns. There has not been as much discussion about the use and misuse of policy towards these minority groups as there has about the westward-flowing Euro-Americans. Native peoples were the inhabitants who were most widely spread across the continent, but Spanish, Mexicans and Mestizos had long cultivated the lands of the southwest, while the French, Métis and Creoles could be found scattered along the waterways and in Louisiana. The Land Ordinance of 1785 recognised native occupancy on what was regarded as land fit for white settlement. The federal government settled treaties with numerous groups on that basis for land transfer. As settlers continued to invade native lands, Indians were steadily moved west of the Mississippi River and then onto reservations or enclosures. Even these areas were subjected to further invasion when the Dawes Severalty Act of 1892 insisted that native groups adopt white individualistic patterns of land holding (Prucha, 1984; Hurt, 1987, pp. 65–153). The sums awarded by the Indian Claims Commission to communities who gave up their original domains are some recognition that native peoples lost their lands unfairly (Lurie, 1978; Prucha, 1984, pp. 2, 1017–23, 1170–9). A vibrant Euro-American western movement pushed aside peoples who were deemed racially inferior and who were considered to use land inefficiently by capitalist standards of profit maximisation. Land policy failed Native Americans.

The claims of other antecedent settlers were adjudicated less peremptorily and with more recourse to judicial mechanisms. Some inhabitants managed to retain their lands or parts of their lands, but others were denied their former holdings. Rights to property were generally deemed to be dependent on documents issued by the predecessor governments of Britain, France, Spain and, after 1821, Mexico. Many of these archival records were incomplete, thereby creating challenges. Perhaps more importantly French, Spanish and Mexican land law differed from that of Britain or the United States. Those grants could be large and were infrequently surveyed; hence boundaries were often vague. Owners rarely confirmed their title as they did in the United States. Under American government sovereignty disputes thus became frequent and lengthy (Hornbeck, 1976; Lamar, 2000, pp. 42–7, 123–35, 424). Historians have argued the rights and wrongs of the adjudication process and of individual claims. Some interpretations have suggested that many residents were robbed because of their language difficulties, their ignorance of American law and the aggression of Euro-American newcomers, but this opinion has not always held sway (Bogue, 1994, pp. 291–2). Other detailed research suggests that both sides made inflated and fraudulent statements. Some residents with large or valuable property hired good lawyers to represent them and substantiated their claims. Yet, equally, government officials without Spanish or French language skills, and having little aptitude for legal particulars, failed to protect the government's interest in disputed land not only against well-paid lawyers, but also against assertive Hispanos (Gates, 1968, pp. 87–119). What is clearer is that the lengthy disputes that ensued were disruptive to local families and had a negative impact on cross cultural relationships and regional development.

Overall, with millions of acres changing ownership and with differing land policies being contested by government officials, lawyers, corporations, entrepreneurs, groups, new settlers, squatters and long-time residents, it is not surprising that there were chicanery, wrangling, errors, mistakes and deceit as well as satisfied owners. But who benefited from the process and its administration will forever be debated. At a macro-economic level it can be argued that the lands were profitably developed, though some sections of land were developed too soon to gain their maximum potential. It seems also that if a model of rational expectations is assumed then the open market system worked in a relatively equitable fashion. Speculators did not disadvantage tenants, who were gradually able to gain ownership (Swierenga, 1977; Haeger, 1986, pp. 35–6). On a political basis, there were many thousands of contented farmers and entrepreneurs who were able to raise their standards of living because the government had offered relatively easy access to land in comparison to their European experience (Gjerde, 1991, pp. 147–50). Yet there were also many unhappy western residents. Many Euro-American pioneers who lacked capital or who were unable to utilise the provisions of official policy found that they could not climb out of tenancy and left the land. Minority residents or racial groups were disadvantaged by inadequacies in American law, by their customs and the colour of their skin. Access to western land was never an even terrain (Bogue, 1994, pp. 288–4).

Land becomes environment

Use or misuse of this land has been analysed more thoroughly in recent years as environmental historians have considered the plunder and preservation of western resources. What contemporary observers perceived as bountiful has increasingly been viewed as misused and wasted. Not only irreplaceable assets like precious and industrial minerals, but also resources that can be harvested, like timber and wildlife, or that can be replenished, like land, have come under historical scrutiny. The effect of climate, especially in terms of aridity, has become central to the west as a region and environmental concerns have featured strongly in recent textbooks (Limerick, 1987; White, 1991; Hine and Faragher, 2000). Furthermore, following the expansion of tourism and outdoor recreation in the late twentieth century, more Americans have become concerned with the preservation of the landscape as beautiful wilderness to be enjoyed and with the history of western tourism. (Wrobel and Long, 2001). As the American west has held a major share of both national resources and spectacular scenery, its record on environmental issues has become significant.

There has always been a tension between the users and viewers of resources. Pioneer settlers and subsequent owners both favoured immediate and direct use and applied machine and information technologies to increase productivity because they were interested in profit and they considered that there was always more land or improved equipment to overcome any deficiencies or problems. Early preservationists thus tended to be intellectuals, often regarded as idealists and scientists. Naturalists like John Jacob Audubon, authors like Ralph Waldo Emerson or Henry David Thoreau and artists like Thomas Cole or Alfred Jacob Miller celebrated the beauty and wonders of nature in the pre-Civil War years. More such 'romantics' who wanted to protect scenery and nature were active in the late nineteenth century. New printing and engraving techniques spread their advocacy of western landscape more widely. Early tourists who travelled west by railroads gave further support in their glowing travelogues and memoirs. Interest groups were slowly building support for nature sanctuaries or what became national parks. The Sierra Club, founded by John Muir in 1892, typified what might be called the early 'Keep America Beautiful Campaign' (Nash, R.,1973, pp. 96–140).

The idealists, however, were voices crying in the wilderness. More important, in the long run, were the scientists who warned about the misuse of resources and challenged the concept of inexhaustibility. George Perkins Nash's volume *Man and Nature* (1864) offered an agenda for land rescue and renewal, emphasising the importance of protecting forests. In his *Report on the Lands of the Arid Region of the United States* (1878), the explorer, ethnologist and geologist, John Wesley Powell, warned that settlers would have to learn to live with water problems on lands west of the hundredth meridian. Carl Schurz was then Secretary of the Interior and he attempted to strengthen and enforce timber regulations. In the 1880s *Forest and Stream* magazine campaigned for wildlife conservation and realistic game laws. Though these voices made little progress in the 1870s and 1880s, they helped create a consciousness about nature and an awareness that better safeguards were needed to protect natural resources. When combined with emerging Progressive reform concerns about efficiency and scientific management, these pressures led to the enactment of public policies to change existing land law and to 'set aside' large sections of the public domain for future use (Petulla, 1988, pp. 225–48).

Environmental politics then became a struggle between those who had long-term vision and those who wanted immediate access to resources. But the ensuing arguments were not always clear-cut. Western states and their representatives felt cheated of the ability to control lands within their own boundaries and protested against federal control in 'Sagebrush Rebellions'. Both eastern and western groups worried about past wasteful exploitation and wanted to harness resources for future use, to scientifically conserve those that could be replenished and to instigate systematic management of federal government lands. Pressure groups lobbied for access to their special mineral, timber, soil or animal interest. Public management bureaus, inefficiently staffed and financed, were accused of failing to discharge their functions, which indeed were at times ill-defined. Trespassing and theft often remained unpunished. From 1891, when the federal government, persuaded by scientific reports, reversed much land policy to set aside forest reserves, there has been intense controversy about the best use of the public domain and government actions to encourage and assist better use of private lands (Gates, 1968, pp. 463–743; Wyant, 1982).

New Western Historians have been vociferous in their condemnation of both public land distribution and private misuse of resources, particularly water. Though earlier historians like Walter Prescott Webb (1931) and James Malin (1947) had taken a similar stance, the modern environmental historians have been strident and loud in their critique of the damage done by pioneers, state and federal governments. The process of westward expansion was in effect a persistent assault on nature that left a legacy of destruction, depletion and death. Donald Worster has often been perceived as the most ardent of the new western environmental historians. Two of his books *Dust Bowl* (1979) and *Rivers of Empire* (1985) passionately analyse the rape of the soil in the southern plains in the 1930s and the major ecological damage that ensued from efforts to redirect water resources in arid lands to western cities. He has continued his crusade to alert the academic world, westerners and the federal government to the havoc caused by environmental changes and has certainly brought a much less positive dimension to the traditional understanding of westerners' association to nature (Worster, 1992, 1994).

He has not, however, been alone. Richard White and William Cronon, both named as New Western Historians, have also brought environmental issues to the fore. Both have written extensively in this area and in the wider developing field of environmental history (White, 1980; Round Table, 1990; White, 1991; Cronon, 1991, 1992, 1994; White, 1994). Though Donald Worster has nailed his colours to a paradigm that emphasises aridity, the hydraulic west and the west as a place, it can be difficult at the general level to distinguish between the thrusts of their work. They all share a common ground of examining ecosystems in relation to their social surroundings and they have all matured as environmental historians to provide more sophisticated and complex treatments than in their pioneering days (Wunder, 1998, pp. 85–90).

Yet it would be a charade to suggest that many other modern western historians have not discussed and enhanced the knowledge of the importance of landscape. Those belonging to the 'gang of four' and whose names are well known have benefited from a wide range of research in the history of western resources. There is excellent scholarship from historians who may not specifically call themselves environmental, but are frequently seen as such by those who practise western history. For example, Donald Pisani has written on both farming and irrigation in California and on reclamation generally in the late nineteenth century; or Dan Flores has contributed extensively to knowledge of wildlife, especially bison on the plains. Other long-established historians like Duane Smith or William Robbins, who have written general or regional histories of resource use, for example, mining and forestry, have long discussed the legacies of land policies and past usage (Pisani, 1984, 1992; Robbins, 1988; Smith, 1993; Flores, 2001).

Environmental history, which emerged in the 1970s and found sufficient supporters by 1976 to begin an academic journal, *Environmental Review*, and a professional society, The American Society for Environmental History, changed the face of land history in the American west. Now increasingly viewed as landscape or resource usage history or what Peter Coates has called 'renatured western history' (Coates, 1994) it has revised frontier history and Old Western History to emphasise the shameful waste and exploitation of resources and the undue distress and misery of settlers. In this the arid lands west of the famous hundredth meridian have become the most highly contested territory.

In some ways the modern recognition of a past bounded by environmental concerns is not new. Many historians recognised the problems inherent in an open market and poorly administered land disposal policy. Many also recognised the instinctive drive for immediate gain in a capitalist system that prioritised private profit over communal wellbeing. What has now been more clearly established is a concern to understand the interaction of nature, climate and people in a sustainable balance (Nichols, 1986, pp. 18–19). The early thrust of this concern was very negative, but recent work suggests that there are opportunities as well as limits into probing into the relationship between humans and the environment (West, 1998; Binnema, 2001).

3
Peoples and migrations

Many people have owned and occupied western lands. All have migrated there. Indeed some have migrated several times within their lifespan, while others have seen their families migrate to another part of the west. Mobility has been a major phenomenon in western settlement and development. Early peoples moved into the west by walking or making some use of animal power to carry either their possessions or themselves, initially on path-breaking routes and then on trails and soft-topped roads. Where natural watercourses were available most people preferred to build a boat – whether, canoe, raft, flatboat, keelboat or barge – for ease and to speed up their passage west. Following technological change steam-driven vehicles were constructed to further accelerate movement. In areas beside navigable water steamboats facilitated settlement, while railroads both enabled land-locked areas to participate more intensively in the market economy and opened up land that other-wise might not have become agrarian. The pace of this human process was relatively slow prior to the advent of steam power. From the early nineteenth century, however, the west witnessed mass migrations as diverse peoples moved in or around its vast dimensions.

Native peoples pre- and post-contact (1492)

Archaeologists and anthropologists are still uncertain about when the first peoples arrived on the North American continent and how they got there. The most common proposition suggests a migration from northeastern Asia during the prehistoric age and then a gradual dispersion throughout the New World which may have begun some 50,000 years ago. It took generations for the first pioneers to establish themselves in specific locations, but perhaps by 1000 AD some groups were settled (Jennings, 1993, pp. 25–82; Snow, 1996, pp. 125–200; Cordell and Smith, B. D., 1996, pp. 201–66; Smith, B. D., 1996, pp. 267–323).

How many native peoples there may have been prior to European contact in 1492 is another contentious issue and may remain a theoretical and elusive number. New World populations have been estimated to range from a low of 8,400,000 to a high of over 100,000,000. Concentrating on America, north of the Rio Grande, the range in the estimates is also extensive, namely from a low of 500,000 to a high of 18,000,000. Few academics accept the extremes of either of these estimates. For America north of the Rio Grande most favour a figure somewhere between 2,000,000 and 7,000,000 (Thornton, 1987, pp. 15–41; Meyer and Thornton, 1988, pp. 5–29; Stiffarm, 1992, pp. 23–54; Krech, 1999, pp. 73–99).

The lack of consensus about the demography of native peoples lies in the debates about how to calculate the devastation of population resulting from disease epidemics which followed the arrival of the Europeans. Certainly native peoples faced severe difficulties in resisting and developing immunities to such contagions as measles, smallpox, cholera and influenza. But some of their numbers may have been depleted following decreased fertility and increased mortality due to malnutrition and starvation in the wake of disease epidemics. The impact of inter-tribal warfare, population relocation, forced labour or dietary changes are unknown. Furthermore, New World populations may not have expanded to the same extent as their Old World counterparts because they did not herd cattle and did not develop an iron technology. There is considerable room for disagreement and discussion in assessing the numbers of inhabitants of North America before 1492. (Thornton, 1987, pp. 15–41, 2002, pp. 68–84; Meyer and Thornton, 1988, pp. 5–29; Stiffarm, 1992, pp. 23–54; Krech, 1999, pp. 73–99).

Whatever the numbers involved, the native inhabitants of the American west were diverse in their settlements and lifestyles. Traditional white encounters, whether descriptive or pictorial have often left the impression of a uniform, savage and primitive people, who could not attain anything close to a civilised status. Since the 1960s anthropologists and ethnohistorians, some of whom have been Native American scholars, have thoroughly destroyed such myopic perceptions and no history of the west now would consider traditional views other than as part of a historiographical tradition. Abundant research on landforms, artefacts, languages and pictographs has demonstrated a broad dispersion of native peoples throughout the continent and subsequent adaptations to manage different climates, landforms, vegetation, cultures and relationships with other native peoples. There were in the pre-Columbian American west many communities differentiated from each other by language, mores and type of livelihood (Snow, 1996, pp. 125–99; Cordell and Smith, B. D., 1996, pp. 201–66; Smith, B. D., 1996, pp. 267–323). Maps of occupation, whether of the Euro-American variety that depict a static landscape marked by tribal names (Map 3:1), or whether of the native variety, where they are pictures of experience produced by the human interaction with the land, point to a highly varied Native American experience that still infrequently features in historical textbooks (Waldman, 1985; Warhus, 1997). Because contact between Europeans and Native Americans rapidly changed the latter's existence it is important to acknowledge the nature and extent of indigenous societies prior to the European encounter.

New Western Historians have been anxious to stress the long and diverse roots of native migrations to and within the American west, but they have been reluctant to cross disciplinary boundaries or even to move between branches of history to examine this past. Discussion of pre-contact Indian population or what Walter Nugent calls 'from time immemorial' (Nugent, 2001, pp. 18–24) still remains in the hands of the archaeologists and a small number of ethnohistorians whose books have been read by those focusing primarily on Native American history and cultures (Jennings, 1993). Regardless of such neglect or the proclivity to academic specialisms, what must be acknowledged is that Paleo-Indians entered and migrated through the New World. Initially they subsisted on large animals, but then became farmers and enjoyed a vegetarian diet. During their settlements and resettlements they developed a large variety of cultures, languages and physical characteristics, often classified, according to ethnologists, as linguistic

Map 3:1 Native peoples of North America.
Source: P. J. Deloria and N. Salisbury (eds.), *A Companion to American Indian History* (Oxford: Blackwell, 2002).

stocks. Within, as well as between, these language families groups could differ widely from each other in customs, beliefs, mode of livelihood and location (Debo, 1970, pp. 9–18; Nugent, 2001, pp. 18–24).

The linguistic stocks, for example, the Sioux, the Comanche, the Athabascan or the Tlingit, recognised by the historians in their texts as groups or traditionally as tribes, were still in the process of change before they encountered European newcomers. But this change was so accelerated as the intruders marched over the lands in search of gold, souls and then empire that it created 'a material and imaginative revolution' tantamount to 'the start of history itself' (West, 1998, p. 33). The Spanish were the first Europeans to investigate the potential of the northern parts of the New World. Moving across and then on to the lands of the American southwest and the central plains from their northern capital of Mexico City in the sixteenth and seventeenth centuries, they brought not only trade goods, new plants, foodstuffs and domesticated animals but also disease, religion and weapons. They first occupied the central areas of New Mexico with their colonising institutions, the *presidio* or military post, the mission station, the *pueblo* or centre of civil government and the *rancho* or large estate. Then in the seventeenth and eighteenth centuries they settled to the east in Texas and Louisiana and finally moved up the coast of California. Though their presence was scattered and at many times was fragile they were a transforming force. They brought new technologies and diseases which altered the land and undermined native lifestyles and economies so that native communities were dislocated and complex patterns of migration followed (Weber, 1992).

Historians initially neglected but have now, in the wake of the rapid expansion of Mexican population in the Southwest, passionately debated the impact of the Spanish-Indian contact zone or Spain's North American borderlands. Missions have been at the centre of much controversy. Though these religious institutions varied across the borderlands, there has been a tendency to pass generalised moral judgements about their impact on native societies. Traditionally interpreted as benevolent and paternalistic educational enterprises in which native peoples could learn European farming techniques and craft skills while living in settled communities, missions have more recently become centres of social and economic control in which native peoples were forcibly reduced to peonage, harshly restrained by a colonial authority and ravaged by European diseases and malnutrition. In turn, this genocide-style of analysis has been subjected to revisionism which wants to give native peoples more agency. But much more work needs to be done before there can be a social history of missions seen from the perspective of the indigenous population or one in which cultures meet with some blending of accommodation and persistence (Weber, 1992; Sweet, 1995; Jackson, 1998b).

Even when religion was not necessarily the main managerial institution, the Spanish continue to be perceived as dark colonisers rather than as mediators of cultural change. Using marriage as a tool of analysis to understand social interaction between peoples, Ramon Gutiérrez recreated a bleak interpretation of Spanish dominance over Pueblo Indian society in New Mexico between 1500 and 1846. The Spanish church, together with the state and the secular elite, used their power, gender and sex to exploit the labour of poorer Hispanics and native peoples. Furthermore they controlled both land and water through intimate social relations (Gutiérrez, 1991). Notwithstanding native agency and resistance, colonialism took advantage and administered mistreatment. Though some critics have commented that such a disheartening interpretation is both selective and a product of its multicultural and politically correct times, it has been very influential in opening up new avenues into a hidden past in which a variety of sources and methodologies can be utilised. Clearly many questions still need to be answered about racial, ethnic and socio-cultural interaction and adjustment during the early colonisation of the Spanish-Mexican rim.

For the native groups who were not as sedentary as the Pueblos and who were less easily subjugated, the Spanish influence in the centre of the continent took a different form. Rather than herding sheep, weaving wool and living in mission stations the more nomadic tribes and those who lived further north took advantage of horses that escaped from Spanish corrals and that multiplied in the ideal environment of the Great Plains (Jennings, 1993, pp. 165–6). Horses were tools of emancipation. They enabled plains dwellers to do traditional work such as hunting and gathering much more efficiently and they facilitated the expansion of their trading networks. Horses were much better beasts of burden than were dogs. But horses had other advantages. Once plains' nations became skilled equestrians, horses increased the mobility of those groups who had enough animals for all their members. They permitted their owners to move further and faster, not only changing habitats, but also creating tension and competition between groups. In addition horses became commodities as well as liberators. As valuable property and signifiers of wealth and status, horses became objects of desire, thereby stimulating raiding and intertribal conflict. The Spanish legacy of the horse on the plains was one of expanded power and choice and one of mobility. This, in turn, led to disequilibrium in an area where essentials were often in short supply. Numerous groups abandoned their former way of life to become nomadic hunters on either a temporary or permanent basis (West, 1998, pp. 49–58; Krech, 1999, pp. 135–6).

The Spanish were not the only European nations to create new patterns of livelihood and migration among the natives of the American west. English and French colonisers migrated across the continent from the east while the Russians moved south down the Pacific coast. As ambitious mercantile nations looking for trade to consolidate their positions, they considered that North America offered both a passage to Asia through its northern sections and a potential storehouse of natural resources. Though the difficulties of finding easily accessible routes across the continent discouraged major investment in exploratory ventures, fish, fur and lumber proved to be valuable commodities that could be exploited. Exchanging furs and food with native inhabitants for such manufactured products as domestic utensils, trinkets, clothing, alcohol and weapons, was often deemed to be advantageous for both parties. Soon temporary coastal trading posts proved to be inadequate to support such long-distance transatlantic trade and permanent settlements were established. The French dominated in the north, founding communities on the St Lawrence River, then moving to and through the Great Lakes and eventually navigating most of the river systems of the continent. Aided by diverse native groups, they became skilled water travellers, using a variety of canoes and in the course of their extensive journeys they made powerful imperial alliances with natives (Ray, 1996, pp. 46–111).

The English moved more slowly, but they became assertive about building stronger settlements. Starting in the seventeenth century both mercantile and dissident groups came to put down roots on the Atlantic coast. By that time their potential hegemony as colonisers was challenged by the Dutch, the Swedes and the French in the north and by the French and the Spanish in the south. Learning by experience the early English colonial planters found that the native peoples were often friendly and could be helpful for their survival in the difficult first years of adjustment in the unfamiliar environment of the New World. But as they pressed west for more land on which to settle, they came into conflict with both indigenous communities and their European rivals. Negotiating alliances with some native groups was preferable to warfare and the English took advantage of inter-group rivalries to press forward against both other Europeans and native peoples. They learned how to work with existing coalitions and to make new and more advantageous arrangements. They also learned how to realise the gains that could be made because of indigenous population decline caused by epidemics. (Meinig, 1986; Salisbury, 1996; Hine and Faragher, 2000, pp. 39–99).

The interaction of the two major east-coast colonisers, the French and the English, with diverse native communities, whether east of the Appalachians or in the interior of the continent, is now well known as the 'middle ground'. Such interplay between Old and New World peoples that lasted into the late eighteenth and early nineteenth centuries changed both groups and must be understood as part of a process of what can be called 'frontierism'. On a macro level this contact was a repetitive pattern of encounter and intercourse, not in the Turnerian mode of vanquishing the natives and establishing a new American identity, but in a series of complex linkages in which there were many cultural and economic legacies (Cronon *et al.*, 1992, pp. 3–27; Adelman and Aron, 1999).

Native groups made more adjustments than the European newcomers because they were pressured into releasing lands as well as adapting their lifestyles to new trading patterns and consumer products. In migrating to new homes, usually in a westerly direction, they encountered hostilities with other native communities who resisted encroachments into their traditional hunting grounds or their farming habitats. New alliances and accommodations were needed with different native neighbours and new trading arrangements had to be forged with Europeans. These native groups faced both east from the Indian country to engage with large number of Europeans and west from their traditional or perhaps current locations to engage with other groups who, in turn, had been moulded by decades of warfare, disease, migration and resettlement (Richter, 2001, p. 180). The results of these exchanges were visible in ethnic diversity, armed turbulence and an increasing dependency of native groups on trade goods and of Europeans on Indian peoples for both furs and protection (White, 1991a; Sleeper-Smith, 2001).

Seventeenth-century life in the New York/Ontario corridor that straddles Lake Ontario offers an example of the cultural adjustments and the ever-changing political arrangements made consequent on westward-moving European contact with north-eastern woodland tribes. The Iroquois, who lived in lands running parallel to and south of Lake Ontario and were trading with the Dutch, had exhausted the supply of beaver in their homelands and needed to find new sources. They thus raided lands claimed by the Hurons and other Great Lakes nations, sparking a long series of conflicts known as the Beaver Wars. Beaver, however, was not the only resource desired by the Iroquois. They also raided for captives to restock their population, depleted by disease. This intermingling resulted in adaptation of some cultural customs such as the Hurons, who had adapted to French contact, brought Jesuit-style Christianity to their captors. The ensuing tensions were reflected in newly forming political realignments. Traditionalists looked towards the English, who had taken over the Dutch colony of New Netherlands in 1664, while the converted had links with the French in New France.

For much of the late seventeenth century the French, who wished to retain control of the lucrative fur trade of which the Hurons had been a major link, attacked the Iroquois. The English, pushing west for trade and land, offered the Iroquois weapons with which to engage in guerrilla-style warfare with both the French and the nations of the Great Lakes area. They also traded such goods as iron knives and scissors, blankets and textiles, cooking utensils, clothing, beads, tobacco and alcohol which were becoming an important part of the evolving Iroquois way of life. The Iroquois were aware of what was happening and were agents of their own livelihood. The later seventeenth-century adaptation, however, in contrast to earlier changes that had reflected more friendly relation-ships between indigenous peoples and the Dutch saw the Iroquois squeezed between two warring colonial powers and other indigenes, and despite much manoeuvring, they emerged as the losers (Waldman, 1985, pp. 74–8, 93–6, 99; Richter, 1992; Dennis, 1993; Salisbury, 1996, pp. 407–24).

Native communities in the Pacific Northwest also became part of the contested terrain of European colonial rivalry, but at a later date than in either the southern or the east coast regions of North America. Having exploited the fur-bearing animals of Siberia, Russian fur traders and hunters, the *promyshlenniki*, extended their mercantile ambitions to the Aleutian archipelago and then Alaska in the mid-eighteenth century. The Russian maritime penetration of the New World brought change and population decline to two main indigenous groups, the Aleuts, and the coastal-dwelling Indians, the Tlingits. Initially the *promyshlenniki* raided Aleut communities, capturing women and children whom they exchanged for furs. Monopolising the sea otter and seal pelt trade, they left a trail of human damage and destruction. When they ran into competition with the British and the Americans in the 1780s, they established permanent settlements thereby placing greater pressure on the Aleuts to hunt for them and to adapt their lifestyle to foreign invaders. But further south the Tlingits took advantage of imperial rivalries to barter weapons which they used effectively to frustrate the Russian intruders. They also exchanged consumer goods for furs with American and British traders. This exchange created some elements of dependency, though this was not as extensive as in the eastern parts of the continent thanks to geographical isolation. Its greatest impact on native culture came via tools that enhanced the possibilities of woodcarving and the use of trade goods to provide new symbols of wealth that could be used at potlatches (a public sharing of one's goods) to indicate status (Gibson J. R, 1976, pp. 3–31; Gibson, A. M, 1980, pp. 162–81; Waldman, 1985, pp. 124–5).

European imperial rivalries played out on the North American continent were part of an ongoing history of an American west in which migration took new peoples into new lands and forged new identities across the continent. Each wave of migration brought change, both to the environment and to the peoples who were resident on the land. When migration involved changing occupancy or ownership of the land, new settlement frequently resulted in violence (Cronon *et al.*, 1992, pp. 3–27). Once a new American nation, forged from European origins in 1783, claimed much of the land and started to expand primarily westward, the pace of migration and the nature of settlement changed notably in contrast to that of previous centuries. Gone was any notion of coexistence between native peoples and European colonials. For many newly formed Americans, removing natives from the land became part of the national agenda. North America would increasingly become a white rather than an Indian country (Richter, 2001, pp. 189–236).

Euro-American migrations: patterns and contours

Though the British became the dominant colonial power in North America after the defeat of the French in 1763, they were unable to maintain that power when the United States declared its independence in 1776 and had this status confirmed in 1783. Having established a democracy, the new government hoped to attract settlers and to strengthen its position by advertising a greater degree of equality and an abundance of economic opportunity. Migrants did pour into the United States, especially from the late 1840s and many of these followed American pioneers to the lands and towns west of the Appalachians. They were assisted in their migration by the technological advances of the industrial revolution. Steam power, in particular, facilitated movement on both water and land. The migratory process which involved many adjustments and adaptations and which was marked by disturbances and by violence, accelerated sharply after the Civil War. By the early twentieth century a diverse, but dominantly white population, had settled on many of the habitable lands of the west (Table 3:1).

The migration to, and peopling of, the new land proceeded at different rates and in different directions (Table 3:2). As a macro experience, historians have faced considerable difficulties in weaving together the pieces of the rapid, and somewhat erratic, expansion of both native-born Americans and European immigrants into an easily digestible survey. Richard White has commented that any attempt to capture both the broad patterns and the individual events involved in the migration presents staggering difficulties (White, 1991, p. 183). And he, like other New Western Historians, deals only with the region lying west of the Missouri. Yet as he admits there were broad demographic patterns that can provide guidelines for the overall contours of western migration. Such patterns offer a framework for the many more detailed insights of ethnic, racial or family experiences that historians have recently favoured.

The most famous pattern of migration to the American west was popularised by Frederick Jackson Turner in 1893. Though he described this westward-moving flow in graphic prose in his thesis, 'The Significance of the Frontier in American History', the process is more easily understood through the visual representation of the

Table 3:1   Population growth in the west[1], 1790–1920 (in 000s)

Year	United States	Total in eastern states	Total in western states	Percentage of US in west
1790	3,929	3,820	109	1.8
1800	5,308	4,922	386	7.3
1810	7,240	6,162	1,078	14.9
1820	9,638	7,420	2,218	23.0
1830	12,866	9,194	3,672	28.5
1840	17,069	10,692	6,377	37.4
1850	23,192	13,207	9,885	42.6
1860	31,443	15,958	15,485	49.2
1870	39,818	19,412	20,406	51.2
1880	50,156	22,102	28,051	55.9
1890	62,980	28,265	36,715	58.3
1900	84,372	39,648	44,724	53.0
1910	102,370	48,205	54,165	52.9
1920	118,108	55,741	62,367	52.8

Source: The Historical Statistics of the United States (Washington, DC: US Government Printing Office) and *The Statistical History of the United States* (New York: Basic Books, 1976).
[1] The West here is a combined regional approximation (see Table 3.2) and is the equivalent of all regions except New England, the Middle Atlantic and the South Atlantic.

maps in the *Statistical Atlas* of the Eleventh Census of the United States of 1890. Based on the decennial censuses, however defective these were in recording Native Americans and other peoples of colour, the maps point to broad demographic trends (Maps 3:2, 3:3 and 3:4; Table 3:3). Certainly the white or blank pictorial image of the settlement frontier as a place having a density of fewer than two persons per square mile has been discredited. Nevertheless, as a general framework of analysis for ascertaining the dimensions and direction of mainstream Euro-American population growth in the west, it continues to offer reasonable guidelines (*Statistical Atlas*, 1898).

This migration, which contributed the ingredients for the statistical cartography produced by the Census Bureau, was not an isolated phenomenon. As in the years of imperial struggle for the continent, it was connected to broader world patterns of political

Table 3:2 Regional population growth in the west, 1790–1920 (in 000s)

Year	Total west	Great Lakes	(% of west)	Plains	(% of west)	South Central	(% of west)	Mountain	(% of west)	Pacific	(% of west)
1790	109	–	–	–	–	109	(100)	–	–	–	–
1800	386	51	(13.2)	–	–	335	(86.8)	–	–	–	–
1810	1,078	272	(25.2)	20	(1.9)	786	(72.9)	–	–	–	–
1820	2,218	793	(35.8)	67	(3.0)	1,358	(61.2)	–	–	–	–
1830	3,672	1,470	(40.0)	140	(3.8)	2,062	(56.2)	–	–	–	–
1840	6,377	2,925	(45.9)	427	(6.7)	3,025	(47.4)	–	–	–	–
1850	9,885	4,523	(45.8)	880	(8.9)	4,303	(43.5)	73	(0.7)	106	(1.1)
1860	15,485	6,927	(44.7)	2,170	(14.0)	5,769	(37.3)	175	(1.1)	444	(2.9)
1870	20,406	9,125	(44.7)	3,857	(18.9)	6,434	(31.5)	315	(1.6)	675	(3.3)
1880	28,051	11,207	(40.0)	6,157	(21.9)	8,919	(31.8)	653	(2.3)	1,115	(4.0)
1890	36,715	13,478	(36.7)	8,932	(24.3)	11,170	(30.5)	1,214	(3.3)	1,920	(5.2)
1900	44,724	15,986	(35.7)	10,347	(23.1)	14,081	(31.5)	1,675	(3.8)	2,635	(5.9)
1910	54,165	18,251	(33.7)	11,638	(21.5)	17,194	(31.7)	2,633	(4.9)	4,449	(8.2)
1920	62,367	21,474	(34.4)	12,544	(20.1)	19,136	(30.7)	3,335	(5.4)	5,878	(9.4)

Source: The Historical Statistics of the United States (Washington DC: US Government Printing Office, 1975) and The Statistical History of the United States (New York: Basic Books, 1976)

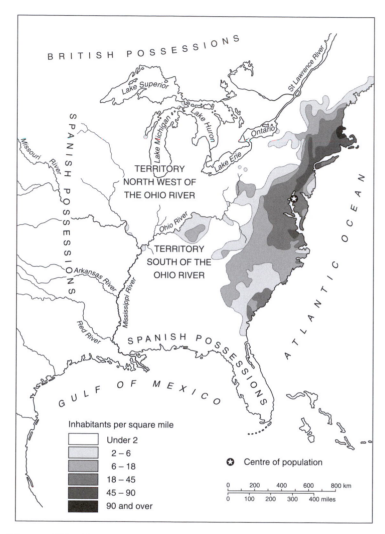

Map 3:2 Distribution of population, 1790.
Source: Eleventh Census of the United States, 1890, *Statistical Atlas* (Washington, DC, 1898).

ambitions. It was also connected to economic fluctuations in the world economy and access to improved modes of transport. Though many historians have preferred to see the American west as a peculiar experiment in democratic development, typecast by

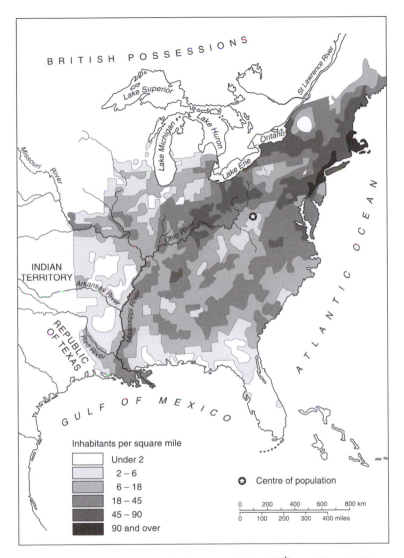

Map 3:3 Distribution of population east of the 100th meridian, 1840.
Source: Eleventh Census of the United States, 1890, *Statistical Atlas*
(Washington, DC, 1898).

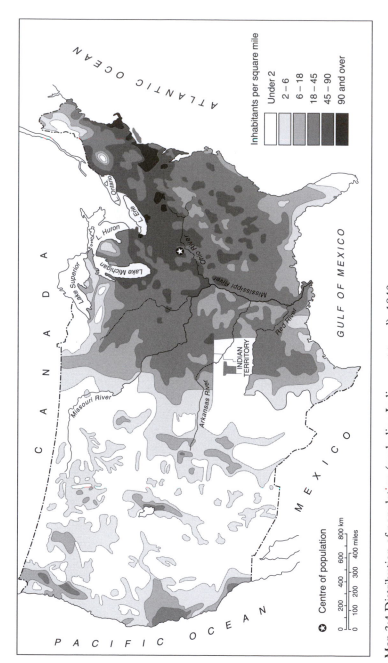

Map 3:4 Distribution of population (excluding Indians not taxed), 1840.
Source: Eleventh Census of the United States, 1890, Statistical Atlas (Washington, DC, 1898).

Table 3:3 Position of centre of population in United States 1790–1890

Year	West longitude	Approximate location by important cities and towns	Western movement in miles during preceding decade
1790	76° 11′	23 miles E. of Baltimore, MD	–
1800	76° 56′	18 miles W. of Baltimore, MD	41
1810	77° 37′	40 miles N. W. by W. of Washington, DC	36
1820	78° 33′	16 miles N. of Woodstock, VA	50
1830	79° 17′	19 miles W-SW Moorefield, W. VA	39
1840	80° 18′	16 miles S. of Clarksburg, W. VA	55
1850	81° 19′	23 miles S. E. of Parkersburg, W. VA	55
1860	82° 49′	20 miles S. of Chillicothe, OH	81
1870	83° 36′	48 miles E. by N. of Cincinnati, OH	42
1880	84° 40′	8 miles W. by S. of Cincinnati OH	58
1890	85° 33′	20 miles E. of Columbus, IN	48

Source: Eleventh Census of the United States, *Statistical Atlas* (Washington, DC, 1898), p. 11

the very name frontier, and peopled by freedom-loving individualistic migrants, this west cannot be dissociated from links to Old
World empire-building and economies (Webb, 1951, pp. 1–28;
Nugent, 1989). The capitalist governments of western Europe
were well aware that their developing industrial economies could
be enhanced by developing empires in relatively unsettled distant
lands like Argentina, Australia or South Africa. Though they dir-
ected many of their endeavours through a managerial class who
governed an indigenous working population, their 'colonies' were
also energised by individuals who hoped to gain long-term upward
mobility as a result of their geographical mobility. In this sense the
'mother country' facilitated a political and cultural ethos that
encouraged an out-migration of segments of its population. The
American west, like the colonies tied to their motherlands, was
the beneficiary of such an ethos and its consenting legislative
framework.

This mass migration was stimulated by and, economic historians
would argue, was a result of the economic cycles that have been part
of the maturing capitalist world. European peoples, suffering in the
wake of cyclical fluctuations that resulted in rapid growth followed
by recessions and depressions, were 'pushed' from their homelands.
Increasing population growth put pressure on land availability and
even though many migrated internally to the cities in search of
industrial work, restructuring of land use following technological
changes resulted in human displacement and in starvation. Those
displaced agrarians of the mid-nineteenth century moved primarily
from northern Europe, where the impact of the industrial revolution
and economic dislocation had been felt earlier. On arriving at an
Atlantic coast port those with some capital moved out west using
the water routes of the Erie Canal and the Great Lakes or the newly
constructed railroads. They joined a larger stream of internal
migrants who travelled in the traditional way, using farm wagons
and driving livestock on improved or unimproved roads, as well as
taking advantage of faster and easier modes of transport. For native-
born Americans in eastern parts of the United States, the economic
difficulties of making a living on poor lands provided a stimulus to
migrate to better lands further west as they became available and
safer from attacks by Native Americans. In addition, farmers unable
to provide for all their children encouraged younger offspring to

move to relatively inexpensive land. Only those who were comfortable economically stayed behind (Kulikoff, 1992, pp. 208–25; Bogue, 1994, pp. 279–88).

If the economic changes in northern Europe initially set waves of migration in motion, then the ensuing consequences of these changes both there and in other parts of Europe, now more firmly exposed to the dynamics of technology, had more impact in the late nineteenth and early twentieth centuries. Intercontinental migration accelerated, with many being attracted to the American west. In southeastern and central Europe, displacement from the land and meagre opportunities were assisted by transport technology that had lowered the costs and accelerated the speed of movement. It was possible to buy cheap transatlantic passage on a steamship and to make rail connections to and from that voyage in both continents. Indeed American rail companies actively promoted western opportunities and offered enticements to farm-seeking migrant families to settle on cheap lands (Nugent, 1989; Haines, 2000, pp. 195–201).

Though immigrants were highly attractive potential settlers, domestic residents continued to provide the bulk of western migrants in the years after 1870. Native-born Americans sought both agricultural land on which to build a farm or labouring opportunities in one of the exploitative industries of the growing towns of the west. Both types of migrants made use of the railroad to transport them and in the case of would-be farmers, their belongings and farm equipment, to their destinations. Many farmers, however, still preferred to travel by the cheaper, albeit slower farm wagon, as they were moving shorter distances, often from neighbouring states or in a step-hop fashion from one state further east. Another smaller stream of newcomers entered the Trans-Missouri West from the Pacific ports, adding more ethnic and cultural diversity to the major westward moving stream and the existing antecedent residents. Adding together the migratory habits of both native-born Americans and immigrants to and within the west, some historians have commented that what originated, as an economic move became almost a cultural habit as mobility and high turnover rates contributed to making Americans a nation in motion (Walsh, 1981, pp. 65–6). Demographic fluidity was visible in the eastern as well as the western parts of the country, but the difficulties of western farm building and the instability of early industries and towns within the west contributed much to the wider search for economic opportunity in a fluctuating capitalist economy. Westerners were very mobile.

Their patterns of migration, especially those of the would-be farmers among the native born, were geographically predictable. They were likely to move to areas in the west that were located along a similar line of latitude as the homes they were leaving. The Yankees of New England became Yankee-Yorkers as they crossed the Appalachians and then moved to the northern portions of the Old North West or Great Lakes region. Settlers from Mississippi or Alabama were more likely to move west to Texas than to the Dakotas while those from Illinois or Iowa would head for Nebraska. Traditionally historians often pointed to culture zones and family networking and, in the antebellum years, to the racial issue as embodied in slavery, to explain this phenomenon. More recently historians have combined ecology with the rational economics of maximising the value of human and physical capital as an explanation. As most migrants went west to farm and as many were already farmers, they took their plant seeds and work animals with them and made use of their knowledge of such conditions as particular soils, seasonal rhythms and specific crops. For example, when seeds are moved to another latitude, where the seasonal changes in light are different, plant productivity drops. Migrants thus tended to have a better chance of starting a successful farm if they remained close to the latitude of their place of origin (Steckel, 1983; White, 1991a, pp. 184–5; Atack, Bateman and Parker, 2000, p. 324).

Though longitude became more important when native-born Americans moved into the arid lands west of the ninety-eighth or hundredth meridian and lacked experience of such conditions, they could still be assisted in their endeavours by European farmers moving along parallel lines of latitude. Conditions in the American plains were similar to those in Eastern Europe and immigrants brought seeds and knowledge about their use with them. For example, the Mennonites introduced foreign strains of wheat, like Turkey Red to Kansas and Nebraska in the 1870s while the hardy spring variety grown in northern Europe was more suitable in Dakota Territory further north. Adjustments still had to be made in adapting such wheat strains and developing a satisfactory milling process, but the factor of familiarity eased the initial adjustment to new lands (Bogue, 1994, p. 299).

Another apparently contradictory contour visible in the migration and demography of the west is the lack of a uniform pattern for the area as a whole. The Turnerian perception of westward migration tends to offer a picture of a west steadily infilling from older settled parts of the country and from Europe, and also having an agrarian profile. What was good enough for Wisconsin and Iowa was good enough for the rest of the continent. But the leap-frog migration by overland trail and by sea to the Pacific coast in the mid-nineteenth century does not fit such a description. The recognition of Far Western difference is not a new proposition, though recently it has been made to look as though it was. Well before the New Western Historians asserted their regional boundaries for the west, other historians were claiming that the Pacific and mountain areas had developed economies and societies that defied a steady demographic or agrarian inflow (Pomeroy, 1965).

Early Pacific coast settlements were built round extractive industries such as mining or lumbering. As such they developed a boom and slump pattern of migration and growth that was often centred on makeshift towns and a demography that was predominantly male and often highly diverse in nationality. Though some of the mineral wealth and the lumbering activities had a durable character that stimulated permanent urban growth and there were opportunities for farming and commerce offering stable prospects, settlement in the nineteenth-century Far West needs to be seen as the result of a migration that was different from the mainstream pattern. It may bear some superficial resemblance to the advance and retreat of pioneer farmers in the more arid lands of the Plains West (Shannon, 1945, pp. 307–9), but until the Far West was connected by rail to the rest of the country and could produce commodities capable of bearing the cost of long-distance rail freight it offered a distinctive demographic profile.

Part of this distinctive profile was connected to family, age and sexual structure as well as to temporary or permanent settlement. Recent discussion of these personal ingredients has not only altered the contours of the Far West, but has completely undermined the traditional approach to mainstream westward migration. For well over a quarter of a century social science historians, women's historians, family historians and rural historians have discredited one of the traditional notions about migration, namely that young white males populated the west. Such a vision may well have suited the male historians of the early twentieth century and may have been perpetuated by the Hollywood film makers who have preferred romance to reality, but it has been unable to withstand the countless criticisms of the new generation of historians who emerged in the liberal years after the Second World War.

In the 1960s social science historians and quantifiers substantially weakened the white male framework of frontier migration. Probing much more systematically into theoretical frameworks than had Turner's generation of interdisciplinary scholars and taking advantage of the technological benefits of computers to analyse and quantify empirical data, they measured the demography of the newly settling west, often in minute detail. Their case studies were centred on the same source that Turner used, the decennial census; only they frequently used the manuscript version to provide the records of individuals that were then codified for computerised analysis. They supported their quantification with a range of other local sources such as letters, diaries, newspapers, travelogues and biographies and they looked to their peers to corroborate or disprove their findings, thereby hoping to make general and testable propositions. Though highly significant on a micro-level in demonstrating that the west, or more frequently in their research, the frontier was peopled by women as well as men, by children as well as adults of a variety of ages and by a mixed group of white people who might more correctly be called Euro-Americans together with some peoples of colour, their findings did not lead to a demographic analysis of western migration (Walsh, 1981, pp. 55–6). The results were both too few and too diverse to be welded together into a systematic overview.

Indeed diversity became the buzzword in understanding the demography of the new country. Women's historians had a field day in knocking down the male framework where women had been either invisible or were stereotyped as long-suffering, dauntless or deviant persons. The quantitative studies of population had already pointed to an abundant female presence and photographs amply substantiated this numerical evidence. Women's historians, however, dug through and found new and other written sources to demonstrate that women were essential to economic survival and well-being in all movements to agricultural areas. There they were part of a family pattern in which they raised and cared for children, ran homes and worked as labourers. Single women also migrated to the west. Though fewer in number than their married counterparts, they were able to find work in the limited number of gender-typed occupations available in the nineteenth century. Women's services were in high demand everywhere. This ensured that there was a female participation in populating the west and one that was worth discussing (Walsh, 1995).

Age failed to acquire as much attention in deconstructing the dominant white male image of the general pattern of migration, but there have been some significant findings. Traditionally youth was regarded as one of the keystones to surviving pioneer hardships and to producing the offspring needed to work on a farm. But such youth was deemed to be in the prime working age between fourteen and twenty-five. Migrants of a younger age were ignored or marginalised. Yet evidence abounds in census records, diaries, memoirs, church records and school buildings that children moved west. They were visible on the overland trails to Oregon and California, whether getting into difficulties or being supportive in trail tasks. They were needed on the pioneer farms. As these farms were often relatively isolated, children were valuable assets who could share small household chores around the farm like fetching water or feeding animals and then, from around the age of ten, who could undertake larger jobs by joining their fathers in the fields. Children were also notable in the emerging urban communities where they helped in stores, hotels and restaurants, attended school and played games (West, 1989; Hampsten, 1991; Craig, 1993; Werner, 1995). Children were certainly a part of the migratory process, though how large a part it is difficult to ascertain.

Peoples of the American west

The migratory flows of native-born Americans, immigrants, men, women and children merged with the native peoples, the remaining colonials and the persons of mixed European and indigenous ancestry already resident in the west to form a cosmopolitan society.

Frequently this was neither an easy nor a smooth encounter and has recently been called an invasion or a conquest (Limerick, 1987). For New Western Historians racial minorities were frequently exploited and mistreated and Native Americans were stripped of their lands and corralled on reservations. Yet numerical dominance did not necessarily ensure a uniform Euro-American supremacy. White native-born Americans fought with each other over issues of land, mores and religion as well as patronising and exploiting those whom they deemed to be their social inferiors. European immigrants faced difficulties with language and culture in trying to adjust to American ways. They often, but not always, found themselves at a disadvantage. More attention needs to be given to the complexities of the Euro-American experience as well as to establishing the agency, resistance, victory and defeat of 'others' or minority groups. The multicultural experience, so lauded as a progressive model of social relations in the twenty-first century, needs much more analysis of all its constituent parts in the years of settlement and early growth of the west. But, as with earlier case studies produced by social science historians, the findings may be too diverse to make general statements. Discussion of fragmented groups may be the best way forward to understanding the diverse roots of 'a west of in-migrants' as distinct from a nation of immigrants.

Any examination of a past multicultural west should start with the most maltreated, but the oldest group of residents, the Native Americans. Here historians have been faced with examining the clash between two occupying or 'would-be' occupying 'nations'. In the overall picture there is little doubt that whatever agency and decision-making power Native American communities held, individually and collectively, they became casualties of an aggressive white culture and an expansionist government who could not or would not control westward-moving settlers. Looking again to the east rather than from the east, the numerous native-language families and their sub-groups saw their lands seized and occupied by avaricious settlers, supported by a government anxious to develop a national economy and apparently willing to overlook or neglect many considerations of human decency. Economic incentives aided and abetted by a white racism that could not come to terms with cultural difference condoned the theft of land and sanctioned the detention of natives on smaller and smaller areas known as reservations.

Liberal historians have long criticised the behaviour of both the federal government and westward-moving migrants. It did not take the advent of New Western Historians to recognise injustice, even though traditional texts were couched with qualifications and rational explanations of white actions. The forceful and brutal 'conquest' was visible for any reader to comprehend; but this conquest was traditionally perceived through one-dimensional spectacles. Before the 1960s those who wrote about Native American history, then more commonly called Indian history, described events and policies from their position as onlookers who relied on conventional written evidence as their main sources (Billington, R. A., 2nd edn 1960). Later historians, who also used written sources, portrayed federal policy and the actions of incomers, whether settlers or the army, with a more judicious eye and they carefully scrutinised the dilemmas facing the lawmakers, law enforcers and the humanitarians (Prucha, 1984; Utley, 2003). Their studies sought to be dispassionate. But, as their contemporaries were products of the age of equal opportunities and their successors were the products of political correctness, so their thoroughly researched histories of treaty-making to obtain land, official 'Removal' policy, wars, guerrilla and formal, missionary activities and the work of the government's bureaus and their Indian agents seemed more like defences of an unjust and avaricious colonial power than an explanation of the arrangements following contact and interaction between two differing nations.

Other well-researched and detached interpretations have received less negative attention. Set in a differing context, namely that of membership in a new nation seeking its identity, the changing residence and status of Native Americans in the west has been interpreted as an assimilation dilemma. In this it has some correlation with the broader political issues of the adjustments of immigrants. Assuming that most Americans in the early years of the republic considered that their society should become a homogenous nation, then any newcomers or existing antecedent settlers must be assimilated. Assimilation then meant some social norm defined by Protestant and Anglo-Saxon standards of behaviour and an ideal that would eventually result in citizenship for all who abandoned their primitive or non-conformist ways. By the end of the nineteenth century when many more diverse newcomers were entering the

United States, policy makers recognised that such aspirations were outdated and they revised their goals to envisage a nation in which some persons were more equal than others (Hoxie, 1984). There would be first-class citizens and second-class citizens with the latter being granted partial rather than full rights. Any non-white minorities would be inferior peoples. Not until the civil rights movements of the 1950s and 1960s challenged this ideal, did the political culture of the country sanction equal rights legislation for all regardless of race, sex or religion.

Such an interpretation gives some credibility to politicians, philanthropists and missionaries who knew they faced a cultural dilemma in finding a means of reconciling major differences between native peoples and Euro-American newcomers. They understood the latter's capitalist desire for upward economic mobility and also accepted that the cultural gap, let alone the racial difference between the newcomers and the native residents would need to be resolved by a period of adjustment. Separation, education and religious instruction seemed to be the most humane solution. This would be a temporary situation. But the relentless push of Euro-Americans westward and the influx of immigrants from a range of European countries changed the political agenda. In the west there were fewer and fewer lands on which the native peoples could be isolated and trained for civilisation. Furthermore, the government and private agencies lacked the commitment and enthusiasm to invest the personnel and capital to civilise reservation inhabitants, let alone to overcome their resistance to efforts to change their ways of life. In the east there were more and more migrants from other parts of Europe who did not fit the ideal of full or immediate citizenship. They looked different from and seemed to behave differently to earlier immigrants. At this point any egalitarian ethos on the part of policy makers disappeared and they reneged on their earlier promises to change and assimilate native peoples and to provide equality. Within the welter of poor treatment meted out at the hands of the government and its agents to those who were constrained on reservations there was at least a period of time in which it looked as though official policy had some redeeming features (Hoxie, 1984).

Yet for many 'New Indian Historians' there is little if anything positive to be said for government or Euro-American relations with natives. The conjunction of ethnohistory, as a discipline founded by anthropologists and historians, the growth of 'Red Power' activism and the founding of Native American Studies programmes in the 1960s and 1970s created a climate in which it was necessary to understand native peoples from their perspective. There was a need to know what was going on (Edmunds, 1995, pp. 724–5). How did the Cherokee feel about their enforced migrations to Oklahoma in the late 1830s? How did communities like the Arapahos, Cheyennes or Crows respond to the 1851 Treaty of Fort Laramie that attempted to establish peaceful relations, assigned boundaries for the territory of each group and provided for annuities? How did Sioux groups react to returning to agencies and reservations to share these with other communities after their attempts to return to their former lifestyles failed in the 1870s? Some partial answers to such questions may be located in the work of ethnohistorians, in native narratives and in post-modern or post-colonial studies that blur boundaries and like to develop ambiguities (Edmunds, 1995, pp. 737–9; Deloria, 2002, pp. 13–21). The presence of native peoples in the west has yet to be fully developed, let alone impartially discussed.

The presence of peoples of mixed native ancestry in the American west, however, needs to be recognised before it can be analysed. Though relatively small in number these ethnic groups occupied a distinctive place that indicates past inter-relationships and a demographic pattern that should not be ignored. Two such mixed communities have received attention since the new social histories have emerged. The Métis were of mixed native and European, usually French, ancestry. The Mestizo were of mixed Spanish descent (Brown and Schenck, 2002). The Métis developed a much stronger identity in western Canadian history than in their American counterpart, but recent work on the Great Lakes area has clearly demonstrated that the French intermarried with native women there and populated trading settlements which provided important links to diverse other communities (Murphy, L. E., 2000; Sleeper-Smith, 2001). French fur traders also cohabited with native women in the Mississippi and Missouri River Valleys. Their offspring were often raised among native communities and have thus not been perceived as having a specific identity (Brown and Schenck, 2002). Their hidden presence may also be partly a result of the difficulties that both the American government and American pioneers faced in recognising racial diversity. In the southwest portions of the United States the Spanish contact with native peoples, resulted in a Mestizo population. During Spanish occupation the Mestizos were an acknowledged part of western society but they, like mulattoes, native groups and African Americans, were socially inferior to Hispanics on account of race (Weber, 1992, pp. 326–8; Brown and Schenck, 2002, pp. 333–4). Demographically, however, they too demonstrated that ethnic pluralism has long standing.

The Southwest hosted another mixed race migratory people, the Mexicans, who added to the ethnic features of the American west. Of Amerindian ancestry, a combination of Native Americans, European Spaniards and African Americans, Mexicans were both antecedent residents when the United States annexed lands from Mexico in 1848 and they subsequently migrated north across the long Rio Grande boundary. Estimates suggest that there were about 80,000 Mexicans in the Southwest in the 1840s, the majority of whom lived in New Mexico. They were primarily farm labourers either on their own small irrigable holdings or workers on the *rancheros*. A thin tier of lighter-skinned *ricos* or *tejanos*, who claimed to have more Spanish blood, held large estates and dominated political arrangements until they were displaced by incoming Anglo-Americans who knew how to use the new political and legal system to advance their position.

Under American rule Mexican workers were exploited not only as peons on land, but also as immigrant miners through the Foreign Miners Tax of 1850. Race as well as lack of skills, or in the case of miners, presence of skills, was at the root of social and economic discrimination. Indeed the history of Mexican peoples in the American west in the second half of the nineteenth century can best be described as separate and inferior. Though there were marked differences within the Southwest, depending both on the numerical presence of Mexicans and that of incoming Anglo-Americans, and rural population started to move to cities as the railroads spread through the region, discrimination and subordination was paramount. By the turn of the twentieth century there may have been some 400,000–500,000 persons presumed to be Mexican in the region, but how many were native-born and how many were immigrants or second generation is unknown. There was a growing demand for cheap unskilled labour on the railroads and on the large farms whose seasonal fruit and vegetable harvest could now be transported to eastern markets (Limerick, 1987, pp. 235–51; Paul, 1988, pp. 139–57; Peck, 2000, pp. 40–6; De Leon, 2002). Newcomers and long-time residents were an essential part of the economy and were creating a cultural landscape, but were marginalised politically and socially.

Native peoples, mixed native groups and Mexicans were early residents of the American west. Migrants from the east coast, whether domestic or foreign were essentially newcomers, frequently called pioneers. Native-born Americans of European ancestry composed the bulk of the new arrivals and they usually moved west when land had been acquired and surveyed by the United States' government. If these pioneers already held land in older areas, they moved west in the hope of acquiring a more profitable farm. If they were younger children who would not inherit the family farm, they moved west to become owner-occupiers. They often brought farm equipment and livestock with them and thus moved short distances in a pattern of latitude-specific migration and selective settlement. Upland southerners from Virginia and Kentucky went to the southern part of Ohio, but Pennsylvania contributed to the mid-sections of the state while New Englanders were concentrated in the north, below Lake Erie. Similar latitudinal patterns developed in Indiana and Illinois. Notwithstanding differences in individuals and families, these broad sweeps of peoples brought with them a cultural heritage that marked both the initial and subsequent formation of settlement (Swierenga, 1989; Cayton and Onuf, 1990, pp. 25–30; Meinig, 1993, pp. 221–84).

Further west similar patterns of incremental rural migration from nearby states took place. Now, however, some of the east coast traditions were diluted into a Midwestern modification. This adjustment was not so much the result of a Turnerian struggle with the environment in which settlers of diverse backgrounds were moulded into Americans. It grew out of the complex relationship between particular groups, land use and connections to markets. Certainly pioneers did have to make some unanticipated changes following their settlement on virgin or new land, but they often retained their cultural habits for many years, thereby creating district neighbourhoods (May, 1994; Conzen, 1994, pp. 342–51;

Gjerde, 1997). When they moved further west, they retained more of their cultural habits than their specific knowledge of environmental adjustments. Indeed some migrants to areas west of the Mississippi and Missouri Rivers were still considered to be Yankees or Yankee-Yorkers rather than migrants from Ohio or Illinois or even Midwesterners (Shannon, 1945, pp. 38–9; Fite, 1966, p. 36). This classification may have stemmed partly from cultural distinctions still attached to sectional attitudes over slavery or it may have been a demographic issue because the census, which recorded state of birth, made no distinction between the various stages of migration between birth and that census. Such labelling, without recognition of specific origins, contributed to the more generic categorisation of the traditional westward movement as being white Anglo-American. Certainly this rather broad grouping had some allegiance to the English language and an affiliation to common law traditions, but it masked considerable economic and cultural differences which are only revealed by research at the local level.

If the basic label of Anglo-American is not applicable to native-born migration to the rural west, then it is even less appropriate for the comparable migration to western cities and to centres of resource exploitation. American wage earners and wealth makers were a broad-based group. Unskilled labourers, lacking capital or farm experience, moved to a west where they hoped to find employment in the timber and mining camps, on the railroads or as operatives in processing factories. They came from both the farms and the growing cities of the east and sometimes from western farms, worked on a temporary or seasonal basis and did not leave a specific cultural imprint (Schwantes, 1987). As a mobile work force their presence has been hidden other than in a quantified format presented at the micro level. Merchants and businessmen working in eastern cities sometimes migrated to set up branch activities of established houses in the new western centres like Chicago, Kansas City or Omaha. At other times individuals, who saw the west as a growing area, took their savings west to invest in service industries for local residents or in processing for both local consumption and export. Native-born workers, female as well as male and entrepreneurs formed the majority of urban dwellers, whether in a boom and bust type or a permanent centre. Their demographic profiles have yet to be fully analysed.

European immigrants to the American west have been analysed both quantitatively and qualitatively. Historians anxious to give credit to their chosen ethnic group or as part of that ethnic group themselves have sought out diverse language resources and have examined the census records to find detailed evidence of migration and often group settlement. Traditionally much of the research was filiopietistic, or self-congratulatory, in nature and needed some dispassionate filtering. New Rural Historians, however, have adopted a more analytical approach to community growth that has revealed the nuances of immigrant responses to both a new environment and a different culture and language. But their efforts, like those of the traditional immigrant historians have neither effectively acknowledged ethnic group settlement nor recognised the high proportions of European-born pioneers in certain parts of the west. In their multicultural demographic concerns New Western Historians have focused on racial minorities that have previously been marginalised or ignored (Luebke, 1998a, pp. vii–ix). In so doing they have conflated European immigrants with native-born Americans into a mainstream group known as Euro-Americans. These Euro-Americans are frequently perceived to be conquerors, while racial minority groups are victims. Such a perspective is grounded in the equity and affirmative action culture of the post-civil rights era. It should, however, be recognised that European ethnics also played a significant and diverse part in settling and developing the west and also suffered from discrimination.

Statistics from the decennial census volumes and from the *Reports of the Immigration Commission* (1911) clearly demonstrate a significant European immigrant presence in the American west from the mid-nineteenth century. In the pre-Civil War years large numbers of European farmers migrated to the newly settling states of Illinois, Wisconsin, Michigan and Iowa while other immigrants went to the emerging cities of the Great Lakes and the Upper Mississippi Valley. For example, two years after Wisconsin became a state in 1848, the census recorded that a third of its population of 305,390 was foreign-born. Many European newcomers who had some capital were agreeably surprised to find that land ownership in the west was relatively easily accessible. Others found economic opportunity and personal refuge in the growing ethnic urban enclaves.

In the post-Civil War years European immigrants moved west in even greater numbers contributing to settlement and growth. A quarter of Nebraska's population of 123,000 in 1870, a third of California's population of 865,000 in 1880 and a third of North Dakota's population of 319,000 in 1900 were foreign-born. Expanding the statistics to include second-generation immigrants, the proportions of ethnic population in some areas of the Plains and Mountain West become much higher. For example, the Dakotas were very attractive to foreign-born persons who wanted to farm. In 1900, 71.3 per cent of North Dakota's population was either first- or second-generation immigrants, while the comparable percentage in South Dakota was 57.6. But in the Rocky Mountain states immigrants also moved to the mines. In Montana 50.6 per cent of the population was composed of immigrants and their American-born children; in Colorado the comparable figure was 37.3. There the dominance of Scandinavian, especially Norwegian settlers declined, though Germans continued to spread throughout the region. Irish, English and Canadian immigrants were also attracted in significant numbers to the opportunities west of the Missouri River (Luekbe, 1998a).

Statistics, however, are not as important in recent interpretations as are the cultural and social experiences of either individuals or groups. For those historians who are anxious not to have the European experiences diluted into something amorphous called Euro-American, community studies have been the way forward to re-evaluating the ethnic history of the American west. At times these studies and their authors have not been perceived to be part of western history. For methodological reasons those who have retained an interest in quantifying as well as analysing culture have affiliations with the New Rural History (Hahn and Prude, 1985; Clark, 1991; Barron, 1993). Equally other historians whose work has examined rural life have preferred to be identified with the broader revitalised immigrant history (Conzen, 1990, pp. 308–9). On geographical grounds several path-breaking studies have focused on part of the Midwest or the Old Northwest, areas that do not feature within the regional bounds of New Western History. Yet, whatever their nomenclature, the contributions of these studies are significant to understanding the multicultural past of the west and to developing an inclusive history that also reflects diversity within whiteness.

The contributions of and adjustments made by German immigrants have featured strongly in the new and specific community approach and can point to ways of enhancing the account of a diverse western past. Germans migrated to the American west since colonial times. There was, however, an upsurge in numbers in the late 1840s and a continuing flow throughout the remainder of the nineteenth century, peaking in the 1880s (Conzen, 1980, pp. 405–11). Looking at both the rural and urban contributions of German immigrants and their children in St. Martin's Township in Stearns County, Minnesota, and in Milwaukee, Wisconsin, Kathleen Conzen has amply illustrated that ethnic experiences involved cultural contributions as well as environmental adjustments. Understanding the European background was very pertinent to understanding the ways in which ethnic communities transmuted and evolved. In pioneer St. Martin's Township German immigrant farmers and their children maintained and revitalised family values by adapting their traditional mores. Though responding positively to the commercialisation of agriculture, they developed a complex set of strategies to ensure that their children had an early start in farming, that all children were treated equally and that early retirement would keep the land in the family. In pioneer Milwaukee the Germans were neither completely assimilated into nor excluded from American culture. They adjusted to the political and economic milieu, but developed their own alternative community with its institutions and activities (Conzen, 1976, 1985).

On a macro level the American west was dotted with ethnic island communities. In Dalesburg, a farming community on the eastern fringes of the Great Plains in South Dakota, Swedish immigrants built a community that was shaped by networks experienced in the common migration from Europe. Some farmers travelled directly to Dalesburg, but others moved there indirectly through other Swedish communities in Illinois, Wisconsin, Minnesota and Iowa. These links with other places together with kinship ties, streams of information and religion were important in creating and maintaining social and cultural enclaves in many settlements in South Dakota. For example, in the early twentieth century, rural Norwegian, German or German-Russian communities were quite parochial and inward-looking socially, though their farmers adapted more rapidly to American patterns of economic behaviour.

The degree of ethno-cultural persistence varied both between specific groups and specific location of settlements and this variety makes generalisation difficult (Ostergen, 1983, 1998). But it also points to the complex nature in the whiteness of rural society in the west.

Gone is the traditional Turnerian hypothesis of a frontier melting pot with its easy rural assimilation process. The broader picture too, is one of diverse ethnic history gradually emerging from the interaction of culture and environment. There was an ethno-cultural evolution. In the upper Midwest, ethnic European farmers, whether German, Norwegian or Swedish, did not imitate their American counterparts. Rather they lived in a state of tension with their native-born neighbours. The ensuing social and religious modifications translated into new and often divergent patterns of culture and beliefs. It was possible to blend in with a dominant culture, at the same time as maintaining ethnicity despite that dominant culture (Gjerde, 1997). This thesis of modified cultural pluralism merging localised non-Anglo immigrant culture with regional and national economic, social and political participation has set the agenda for redrawing the rural west.

In some ways that agenda had already been attained by urban immigrant history, which had been revitalised in the 1970s by adopting the methods of the new social history. The questions that were then being asked and the methods used were extended to western cities, and their ethnic enclaves came under scrutiny. There, too, immigrants adapted some of their cultural values while adopting American political and economic habits. The Irish, who were numerous in the mining areas, were a case in point. In Butte, Montana, one of the most overwhelmingly Irish cities in the country, with a quarter of its population either Irish-born or second generation Irish, the men adopted exclusionary tactics to protect and distribute mining jobs and formed welfare associations to provide against the hazards of the job. They and their families preserved Irish traditions through such institutions as ethnic associations and the Catholic Church and through such activities as St Patrick's Day celebrations, celebration of death via wakes and a saloon habit. In the copper smelting town of Anaconda similar adjustments took place as Irish men created a niche for themselves in the workforce while the women transplanted and then shaped traditions in the homes and joined men in organising ethnic associations, essential for mutual aid (Mercier, 1997; Emmons, 1998a, 1998b; Mercier, 2001, pp. 9–44). Some aspects of Irish identity were preserved into the second and third generations, leaving a distinctive ethnic contribution to western mining communities in Montana. These adjustments need greater recognition in the history of the American west.

The presence and reception of, as well as the adjustments made, by African Americans in the west have been acknowledged since the civil rights era insisted on making black Americans not only visible, but also agents of their own lives. It is now fully recognised that African-Americans added a colour component to the dominant white westward-moving population in the nineteenth century. As both slaves and free people, female and male, they participated as workers and contributed to settlement as a distinctive and separate category of people (Taylor and Wilson Moore, 2003, p. 24). Though there is still no complete history of African-Americans in the west because of the need to undertake more local studies, historians suggest that the black experience is most appropriately categorised as paradoxical. The relatively modest population recorded in the census implies that African-Americans did not consider that the west offered better opportunities than elsewhere in the country. Racism was prevalent in many parts of the west and distance from other black communities might have also discouraged relocation (Taylor, 1996, 1998). Yet African-Americans both as individuals and as groups found that they had more opportunities both to live as they chose and to gain a measure of success in the west (Billington, M. and Hardaway, 1998, p. 5). In uncovering the complex layers of black American lives historians have also been concerned to deconstruct the mythical imagery of the rugged black cowboy, the gallant Buffalo Soldiers and the sturdy, but silent black women. Such stereotypes of the black westerner established by earlier writers have created idealised notions rather than produced evidence about people (Taylor, 1998, pp. 2–3). That evidence of actual black experiences has now become more visible. What now needs to be discussed in greater detail is how African-Americans interacted with other groups in the west and how they adopted new customs and defined their identity as a minority people (De Leon, 2002, p. 107).

Chinese immigrants had less opportunity than African-Americans as a racial minority group and even less opportunity as an ethnic community to adapt their traditions to American life. Arriving in the mid-nineteenth century, most hoped to be temporary sojourners, earning enough to return home with an improved standard of living. By far the majority were men who had left their families behind and of those who came to California most relied on the credit-ticket system, paying off their loan and its interest out of their earnings. Very few women migrated to America; only accounting for some seven per cent of the Chinese American population throughout the late nineteenth century. On arrival in the United States many became prostitutes. Chinese communities were thus composed of disjointed households. Most men lived in crowded conditions with their social life focused on clubs, temples, opium dens and brothels. Their societies and associations did provide some communal life and gambling and the celebration of religious festivals remained an integral part of Chinese culture, but the Chinese often remained separate from other groups in the west. The continued wearing of oriental dress and the pigtail and the unusual nature of the Chinese language strengthened the American view of them as an alien group. Nevertheless Chinese labour was essential to the western economy in mining, building railroads, running restaurants and laundries and farming. But the Chinese were not allowed to work unhindered. The Foreign Miners Tax of 1852 had adverse repercussions and subtle local ordinances, such as the laundry-related ones of San Francisco impeded their livelihood. Furthermore, other workers were hostile because they considered that the Chinese were stealing their jobs. To add insult to injury the Exclusion Act of 1882, renewed ten years later, barred further immigration. The Chinese tested the legality of such laws in the courts, but to no avail. They suffered from prejudice, leastwise in most parts of the west (Paul, 1988, pp. 157–68; Tong, 2003, pp. 19–66). There was less discrimination in Idaho mining districts where the Chinese formed a larger proportion of the camps in the Boise area, but this seems to have been an exception (Zhu, 1997). The Chinese were accepted only on sufferance.

In discussing the peoples of the American west historians have long moved on from examining traditional themes about the speed and direction of male westward movement and the frontier as a process for making immigrants into Americans. They now concentrate on discussing multicultural societies, pointing to the racial minorities who have suffered from discrimination and exploitation. There is no doubt that the west has been a land of many races, many ethnicities and many national origins and that its historians have needed to work with the challenge of understanding the complexity of racism in a society where there was no bi-polar division between whites and others. They have also faced the difficulties of discussing race and minority relations in a situation where discrimination was clearly visible. While most have shown that Euro-Americans used race as a way of ensuring their own privileged status in western society, there have been some differences in interpreting how minority groups responded to this pattern of discrimination. In placing minorities in the centre, revisionist historians have practised a type of affirmative action that ensures that minorities do not suffer from academic mistreatment. Indeed minorities are so central that the white or Euro-American majority has been welded into one large mass rather than its ethnically diverse components. Clearly the demographic portrait of the west has rightly changed its complexion, but the intricacy of racial and ethnic relations and discrimination still has to be thoroughly examined.

4
Making a living:
early settlements and farming

Most migrants to the American west hoped to make their living farming the land. Up to the early twentieth century most western residents were farmers and the rural economy was focused on agricultural productivity. Farmers were, however, more prominent in the Great Lakes, Plains and South Central regions of the west than in the Mountain and Pacific regions of the west and even in the major farming areas some westerners made their living by other means. Some Euro-American pioneers and immigrants moved west early to exploit resources other than the land. They trapped small animals and hunted large creatures. Miners also migrated west. Some hoped to make a fortune digging for gold or silver; others became day labourers working in mines producing both precious and industrial minerals. Yet other migrants sought their living as lumbermen or loggers in the forests. Whether working the land or utilising the other natural resources, the enterprise of all workers stimulated secondary and tertiary activities. Trade and transport connected to the processing and production of resources and services required by those primary producers stimulated the growth of cities and factories. The west then offered diverse opportunities to many and was the workplace of millions more whose lives were governed by the capitalist ethic.

Pre-capitalist 'economies'

It is difficult to talk about native peoples living on the land in pre-Columbian North America in the capitalist terms of market economies forged by the profit motive. They lived primarily in what might be called a subsistence or semi-subsistence world in which they worked to survive and bartered or traded surplus products for items that they were unable to generate themselves. Their exchange also took the form of gift-giving as tokens of esteem, symbols of status or bonds of friendship and obligation. These native economies may seem basic in technological terms as judged by the standards of industrialised nations, but they were sufficiently sophisticated to allow diverse cultures to develop during the course of hundreds and, in some cases, thousands of years. Tools and utensils were crafted from such materials as stone, horn, bone, wood, fibre or copper. The knowledge and ability to store food replaced the sharing of food during shortages and gradually native groups began to practise early horticulture. Then it was possible to develop mixed economies based on cultivated indigenous plants combined with the hunting and gathering of wild foods.

Archaeological evidence may suggest rather than provide definitive evidence of the ways in which the numerous native communities lived and survived during the major periods before contact and in the different regions of North America. Living off the land initially meant hunting and gathering. Native Americans depended on the varied natural food supply of the continent. This included a range of large mobile game species like musk ox, caribou, bison, bear, elk or deer and smaller species like rabbits, racoons, beavers and squirrels. Clams and other shellfish were important additions to diet for coastal groups while a variety of seasonal fish and waterfowl supplied those who lived near rivers, lakes and the coast. The gathering of insects, snakes and lizards, wild plants, nuts, fruits, berries and edible roots and leaves provided both vital and extra sustenance. All hunting, trapping, fishing and gathering was tied into local environments. So the native work regimes and styles of sustenance differed considerably (Gibson, 1980, pp. 21–35; Josephy, 1992, pp. 21–145; Snow, 1996, pp. 144–93).

The Pacific coast peoples of the Northwest from the California–Oregon border through the panhandle of Alaska created primarily hunter-gatherer cultures. They focused on fishing and used the coast and its inlets as a bountiful reservoir. They caught salmon, halibut, shellfish, eulachon (candlefish) and herring, hunted sea mammals, sea otters, seals and whales and gathered seaweed and sea birds' eggs. Using an assortment of technology, including hooks and lines, nets, fish dams and various traps, they could often catch their annual consumption in a few weeks of concentrated activity. Furthermore, there were a variety of plants, shrubs, bushes and trees bearing nuts, berries and fruits and edible roots to supplement diet. The mild climate and abundant rainfall encouraged a dense forest growth of redwood, pine, cedar and fir, softwoods easily exploited and shaped with early tools into dwellings, boats and artefacts. The boats were used for trading with upriver and other coastal groups. With such an abundant food supply and ample materials for constructing shelter, the economies of the Northwestern peoples like the Salishes, the Chinooks and the Tolowa-Tututnis were relatively rich. But they were quite distinctive and geographically separate from populations who developed agriculture (Gibson, 1980, pp. 82–5; Ray, 1996, pp. 15–20; Snow, 1996, pp. 180–3; Fisher, 1996, pp. 117–23).

Domestication of plants had Mesoamerican origins. The native peoples of Central America and Mexico cultivated the land, planted seeds and produced and harvested crops in the years between 5200 and 3400 BC. These early horticulturalists raised corn, beans, squash, cotton and pumpkins. These crops spread across the southwestern portions of the United States, with corn forming the staple foodstuff. In addition, native tobacco was raised for use in ceremonies and for healing. Turkeys were domesticated for food and for their feathers. Successful farming in these arid lands was dependent on irrigation and conservation techniques. Native farmers developed a range of irrigation skills from the simple use of floodwater to the construction of long irrigation canals. Where water was scarce communities used walled terraces and linear borders constructed of rocks to trap and hold water to sink into the soil. With farming supplementing hunting and gathering, peoples like the Hohokam, Mongollon and the Anasazi were better able to develop a more sedentary lifestyle from which to expand their material culture (Gibson, 1980, pp. 26–30; Hurt, 1987, pp. 1–9, 17–26; Cordell and Smith, 1996, pp. 205–13; Krech, 1999, pp. 48–57).

In the woodland regions of eastern North America and in the middle of the continent, Native Americans were slower to move from an exclusive hunting and gathering economy to one in which crops were raised. Changes were made gradually and variably over time and space as the environment evolved. Here plant domestication was independent of that of Mesoamerica. Seeds formed the basis of early horticultural economies and a growing reliance on seed foods and plants encouraged a more sedentary life, which in turn advanced the further growth of farming. Agriculture then moved from botanically diverse garden plots to larger field systems. During this transition corn and beans were introduced from the southwest, with corn increasing and dominating food production in the region after 800 AD. Stone and wooden tools were used in loosening the soil for planting and for harvesting, but no elaborate irrigation technology was needed as in the western parts of the country. Instead peoples in the eastern and central regions learned to develop and adopt varieties of corn that could withstand short growing seasons. Notwithstanding the growing dependency on farming, societies like the Hopewellian, Oneotan and Mississippian continued to hunt, fish and gather plants at different seasons of the year. Their subsistence economies supported a diversity of civilisations (Hurt, 1987, pp. 11–16; Snow, 1996, pp. 146–63; Cordell and Smith, 1996, pp. 234–62; Smith, 1996, pp. 267–77).

The arrival of Europeans on the North American continent imbued by mercantile capitalism may have introduced the ideas of economic profit to native groups, but did not introduce the notions of trade and exchange. These had long been embedded in native cultures either as a means of gaining access to commodities which were not available locally or for social, political, decorative and ceremonial uses. In native societies, people did not accumulate wealth other than as a means of personal or family decoration. They gave it away and gained in stature by showing concern for public welfare. Gifts to individuals and groups symbolised friend-ships and alliances and reciprocity was a cultural requirement. A value of esteem was placed on exchanging items like blankets, pottery, textiles, shells, carvings and some foods. Commerce, whether the extensive variety emerging from Cahokia at the centre of the Mississippian culture or a much more local variety between two neighbouring communities, and whether taking place as a result of warfare or in times of peace, had alternative values to those developed in the Old World. In the words of Francis Jennings, '[i]n terms of economic analysis, goods were acquired for consumption, display and retribution rather than for the creation of capital' (Jennings, 1993, p. 65).

Given alternative cultural norms, there were both misunderstandings and conflicts as native communities traded with European newcomers. Most of the early commerce that followed the arrival of the English and the French was a type of bartering as furs were exchanged for European manufactured goods. The incomers gained natural resources which were sold for profit in Europe; the residents gained manufactured articles that could be both displayed and used. When permanent colonies were established many more adjustments were required and these were dominated by market ideals. Native groups accommodated to more materialistic values and exchange became commercial as well as ritualistic. This greater emphasis on producing surplus commodities propelled native economies from their subsistence to a semi-subsistence basis in which they specialised in trapping furs to gain European goods (Jennings, 1993, pp. 180–5; Trigger and Swaggerty, 1996, pp. 349–61).

As a result of the growing exchange patterns social relationships changed. Within a given community men were more often absent trapping and women took on new tasks as well as processing more skins. Between native communities greater tension arose as they invaded each other's territories in search of animals and, in turn, were played off against each other by rival European or Euro-American companies hoping to increase their commercial output. In this process native peoples cannot be regarded as being naïve traders who were solely victims of imperial greed. They had agency and they learned to negotiate to their advantage (White, 1983; Richter, 1992, pp. 75–104; Trigger and Swaggerty, 1996, pp. 370–89; Krech, 1999, pp. 151–2). But they could not do this systematically as they rarely cooperated with each other to form a more powerful trading bloc. Furthermore, they were depleted by disease, alcohol and warfare and they were outmanoeuvred by superior European weaponry. The interaction of two diverse economic cultures had continuing deleterious consequences on native communities as the stronger European nations and then the Americans pressed for more and more land, considering that land was free because it was not being used according to profit motives. Native groups would be persuaded, bribed or forced, to adjust to and partially or fully, assimilate the habits of Euro-American economies in a lengthy process, and they would rarely gain in this course of action. The economic conduct of native groups has too many cultural ramifications that have not been sufficiently well examined to make categorical judgements about rational decision-making. But the weight of the ongoing arguments in ethnohistory and fur trade history suggests that many were able to adapt to the mechanisms of economic imperialism (Albers, 2002, pp. 276–81).

Varieties of capitalist economies in the American west

When Euro-Americans confronted Native Americans and decided to occupy and develop the vast resources of the continental domain, they brought with them the ideas of mercantile and then industrial capitalism. The abundance of resources and the application of technology to these resources throughout the nineteenth and early twentieth centuries assisted the spread of material values. The American west became a storehouse of burgeoning enterprise and investment and the landscape became a source of wealth (Potter, 1954, pp. 142–65; Robbins, 1994, pp. 61–82).

Traditional historians have interpreted this settlement and development process in a variety of ways. Turner and his followers saw a process of westward expansion in a sequential pattern. The west evolved from primitive to mature status in a sequence that was duplicated as pioneers moved west. What might be called stages of economic growth were chronologically dynamic, but geographically static and did not allow for the intrusion of technological change (Turner, 1893, pp. 1–38). New Western Historians, concentrating on a smaller region have focused on Euro-American capitalist exploitation. This exploitation has been of both the environment and its resources and of peoples of colour. Indeed, a form of economic colonialism was at work (Limerick, 1987; White, 1991a).

There are, however, alternative perspectives on the diverse economies of the west and how residents and settlers lived and made their living. It is possible to link pre-capitalist or North American traditional systems with a modern world system that is based on capitalism in a general approach that gives meaning to a west with a long and continuous past. While models and hypotheses are currently out of vogue because histories are increasingly shaped by the cultural turn, a network of connected points that encompasses the complexity of strands can be linked into a viable interpretation. Mercantile capitalism laid the foundations for an industrial capitalism that encouraged a major rush of varied and competing interests to gain control over resources and profit-making enterprises. Disparate resident and incoming groups interacted in complex ways that involved significant cultural changes and many forms of resistance. These intercultural relations produced many adjustments and adaptations. There were swirls and eddies rather than linear sequences, but these currents were connected to each other and to the broader patterns of global processes (Meinig, 1993, pp. 257–64; Aron, 1994).

Farming and approaches to farming

Most Americans and European immigrants who moved to the west went with the intention of farming. They envisaged that they could acquire some land and build a home and an enterprise. For some pioneers, political philosophers and idealists owning and working land was an end in itself. Inspired by the ideal of the yeoman farmer, it was enough to be a property-holder, have a stake in society and be able to provide a basic living for a family from the land. Most needs could be furnished from the land and there was little to be bought. In other words pioneers could be self-sufficient and would only occasionally produce surpluses for sale in order to buy other commodities. They were part of a rural commonwealth and lacked an interest in improving their economic status by making and accumulating profits (Danbom, 1995, pp. 66–9).

For most agricultural historians such a mindset or a level of living was the product of either an age of philosophical enlightenment or a stage in economic development when geographical isolation and distance from markets prevented commercialised farming. They argued that for many westerners self-sufficiency was a temporary stage rather than a permanent condition. Farmers hoped that they could move from this position and its marginal living standards into production for local markets. Then given access to better means of transport, improved agricultural technology and to some credit or more capital, farmers could participate in agricultural specialisation and regional or national markets. At this point they became more heavily involved in an impersonal capitalism (Walsh, 1981, pp. 31–43).

Such a transition from self-sufficiency into commercialism by millions of America's pioneer western farmers is a well-established historical theme. Most agricultural historians take this as a starting point because they have focused on the economic history of farm production. In more recent years, however, social historians have challenged this materialist viewpoint. When they turned their attention to the countryside they produced a new rural history using different lines of inquiry. Drawing on a number of approaches ranging from the studies of the French *Annalistes* that synthesised all aspects of the rural world, through social science research on the formation of rural communities (Swierenga, 1983), to the new social history with its emphasis on anonymous Americans and human behaviour, they examined people and their behaviour in their locales. Historians of the American colonies initially pointed the way to the possibilities of rural community studies, but it was three articles in the late 1970s that set the agenda and stimulated interest in this approach, as applied to the early national and pre-industrial years of the late eighteenth and early nineteenth centuries. Notwithstanding differences in the range of their topics they all suggested that some, or perhaps many, of the farmers in the northern and western parts of the country in the years before the Civil War did not produce mainly for profit in the market economy (Merrill, 1977; Henretta, 1978; Clark, 1979).

Extending this approach to the west it follows that this area too could be called non-capitalist. The values that predominated would then be those concerned with social relations and sensitivities. The issues that were important were family concerns, communal matters and cooperation and these values shaped a distinctive rural culture. This culture was not a transient phenomenon that faded as pioneers adjusted to their new surroundings and made more local and regional connections. It lasted until the early twentieth century when the arrival of agribusiness threatened the ways in which individuals could contribute to the family and community resources (Neth, 1995).

The concept of self-sufficiency is both an important social and economic ingredient in the debate about the nature of agriculture that took place in the early years of all western settlement. Was the farm unit focused on family life and labour and on neighbourhood networks which provided supportive systems of regular exchanges and social interactions (Neth, 1995, pp. 41–2)? The self-sufficiency here is communal rather than individual and emphasises transactions among neighbours and informal collaborations. Or did significant changes take place in family farming that made links with the impersonal market more important than the local social community? For example, were improvements to the transport system and ownership of labour-saving farm machinery more influential in making farms successful than the help of neighbours at harvest time? Did farmers respond to the incentives of markets, whether urban, regional or national and begin to specialise their production? Or was it possible to both make use of improvements for commercial production and still be part of a bartering arrangement that relied on transactions within the local community? There is no clear-cut answer that states successful farmers became purely commercial while struggling families or those who moved off the land had been 'left behind' by being economically self-sufficient. There were both successes and failures in commercialism and there was a lingering social or rural bonding that was forged in the pioneering years and in times of difficulties.

An important contribution to understanding, though not necessarily resolving the tensions between the approaches of the agricultural historians and the rural historians, has been made through western women's history. The bulk of the enormous quantity of published research has focused on the lives of Euro-American farming women. Using diaries, letters, memoirs, artefacts, photographs and oral interviews, as well as newspapers and organisational accounts of churches, schools and clubs, primarily female historians have been able to recreate the lives and contributions of anonymous women. These women's lives had been previously ignored or discarded by male historians because they concerned daily domestic and household activities and local patterns of social interaction. The findings reveal women's participation in both the economic self-sufficiency of providing food, clothing and welfare and the social community networking of arranging and giving help in times of necessity and providing comradeship on either an individual basis or through a group. They also reveal wives' and daughters' contributions to cash income for a farm and the presence of independent female farmers (Riley, 1988; Jeffrey, 1998, pp. 65–97; Walsh, 1999b).

Women's history has emphasised the need for having more local and community studies of farming and at first sight has strengthened the social interpretations of pioneer and early western farming.

Much research suggests that despite the harshness and isolation of many agrarian experiences many women were robust and practical enough to foster neighbouring activities that helped create a social self-sufficiency that has become identified as a rural culture. Part of this rural culture initially involved economic self-sufficiency or the ability of families to live off the land. But the rural culture remained as a communal value system after farmers produced for markets and did not necessarily conflict with profit motives. Indeed, as farmers became more commercialised, social networking, which was not exclusively feminine, became more organised in groups. It would not be until the early twentieth century that rural culture unravelled under the impact of the gasoline engine, the telephone and the radio, technologies that promoted national values (Walsh, 1999b).

What is more problematic in examining agriculture in the American west is reconciling or deciding to treat as separate the macro and the micro histories. The former tend to become part of national surveys and in recent times have frequently been written by economists or agricultural historians who have more connections with economics than with history. They thus write about themes like labour, mechanisation, profitability, finance, diffusion of knowledge and production in impersonal terms. Rarely does a general appraisal deal with what might be called the social issues of daily life. These are either lost in the sweep of explanations for increasing outputs or are channelled into protest organisations (Hurt, 1994; Atack, Bateman and Parker, 2000, pp. 245–84). The micro histories or community studies frequently encompass details of families' work and spare-time activities, their values and their aspirations, as well as how they accommodated to change (Conzen, 1985; Faragher, 1986; McQuillan, 1990). The current leitmotif of American historical studies, namely diversity, may suggest problems of combining the accommodations made by so many people into an overview that is anything but insensitive.

Farming experiences in the west

Before the 1920s farming experiences in the west are best described as varied. Different types of farms coincided in the same geographical area, whether the Genesee Valley in upstate New York in the early nineteenth century, the prairies of southeastern Wisconsin in the mid-nineteenth century or the plains of North Dakota at the turn of the twentieth century. Not all farmers had the same aspirations to expand or the ability to succeed. Though there was a general move towards specialisation and commercialism over time, some farmers were more ambitious and took greater risks to participate more fully in a market economy. If they did not have access to personal finance with which to buy labour-saving farm machinery then they borrowed money or used credit from local merchants, banks or other financial intermediaries to acquire both technology and land (Doti and Schwekart, 1991, pp. 19–52). Occasionally they were simply lucky. If they borrowed at a time of rising crop prices they were able to pay off debts. Their neighbours, however, were not risk-takers and proceeded cautiously in fluctuating markets. They built their farm more slowly, relying on family labour and supplying as many of their needs on the farm as was possible. They borrowed the more costly machinery in exchange for labour and relied on neighbours for information about new techniques of cultivation and market prices. Natural hazards like drought, hailstorms or grasshoppers could easily result in tenancy, destitution or leaving the land, even though individual states took steps to assist farmers facing crises (Fite, 1966).

Western farmers responded to the challenge of their locality in a flexible way. Some preferred the older ways of immigrants or of transplanted Americans, both of whom were accustomed to a degree of economic self-sufficiency and a sense of community responsibility. Others were influenced by the abundance of the early west, by individualism and by national and international events (May, 1994, pp. 1–8). What rural history has demonstrated in examining western agrarian history is to modify and complicate the traditional positive and wholehearted response to commercialism. It has not, however, overturned the capitalist thrust for profit making (Kulikoff, 1992).

The mid-nineteenth century

Euro-American pioneers, often from the Upper South, moved to the open prairies of Illinois in the second decade of the nineteenth century. By 1830 there was a scattering of households focused on wooded areas along rivers. These farmers brought a tradition of self-sufficiency, producing corn for family and animal consumption, planting a vegetable plot and raising some livestock and a few acres of wheat or other grains for sale. From the early years of settlement into the 1850s farm families helped each other out. They depended on their neighbours to supply a variety of goods, tools and especially labour and they reciprocated in kind. Local artisans like blacksmiths, carpenters, millers and wheelwrights were often paid in kind rather than cash. Economic relations had to be primarily community-based because there was limited access to cash sales. There was little incentive to change what can be described as a rural way of life until transport in the shape of improved roads to Lake Michigan or the Mississippi River and then the railroads through the middle sections of Illinois opened up markets. Improved farm machinery such as ploughs, reapers and harvesters, available in increasing quantities and on a credit basis in the 1840s, speeded up the process (Faragher, 1986).

What proportion of the Illinois prairie farmers responded to the opportunities to enter market production, with what proportion of their land and when, remains unanswerable at the farm level. Economic historians, quantifying data from the census have demonstrated that as a region, or even as a sub-region, Midwestern farms produced large quantities of major staple crops beyond their family needs. This was true for both tenants and owner-occupiers. Most commercialised farms were located in townships some thirty to forty miles from a navigable river, or once rails were built, within a similar distance from the tracks. Farmers could then sell locally, nationally or even internationally. The ability to acquire improved farm machinery or to hire labour was a pre-requisite for this expansion, as family labour provided by women and young children was often inadequate for the heavy physical work. Community exchange mechanisms could also prove to be problematic in the short period in which it was necessary to harvest such commercial crops as wheat. There were struggles in producing for the market, but they were not insuperable and the potential profit was tantalising. Farmers, who disliked what they considered to be the significant risks of ensuring fair prices for their cereals, continued to raise crops to feed their family as well as to sell to market. They then combined the rural and communal way of life by becoming economic actors in a capitalist system. It now appears that northern farmers in the newly settling parts of the west before the Civil War could be both yeoman farmers remaining conservative in their value system at the same time as becoming incipient capitalists motivated by profit (Danhof, 1969, pp. 278–90; Atack and Bateman, 1987; Craig, 1993, pp. 93–105; Davis, 1998, pp. 355–84).

Further west in the mid-nineteenth century the process of 'externalisation' or the turning outward of the farm family, beyond the household and the local community to the world beyond, advanced more slowly (Craig, 1993, pp. 101). Examples from the Mountain and Pacific coast areas suggest that distance from urban markets and lack of improved transport encouraged farmers to remain producing primarily for their families' needs and to develop or retain economic ties within their local community. Migrants who settled in the Willamette Valley of Oregon in the 1840s, in the Utah Valley in the 1850s and the Boise Valley of Idaho in the 1860s, built farming communities before the advent of the transcontinental railroads opened the possibility of national markets. As such they lived in relative economic isolation linked by river and country roads to local urban societies. The differences between these urban societies point to the slow, but ongoing responses to cash sales as profitable options became available. There was a gradual, but unstoppable process of commercialisation regardless of the cultural affiliations of specific settlers (May, 1994).

After a long and tedious overland journey by wagon trail, migrants to Sublimity, Oregon, in the 1840s and Alpine, Utah, in the 1850s gradually built up mixed-crop farms to support themselves and their families. In this they were influenced by their cultural values and aspirations, by environmental conditions and by the local market prospects. The pioneers in Sublimity, like those in other early communities in Oregon had already practised the habits of small farmers where household production, kinship relations and self-sufficiency dominated. They found that in the temperate climate of the Willamette Valley it was possible to raise cereals, vegetables and livestock, though not in the same mix as in the Upper South or in trans-Appalachia because of environmental conditions. Some Sublimity farmers raised crops for sale in Salem or Oregon City. In this they were following the example of earlier farmers who had supplied the fur trading posts of the Hudson's Bay Company. Some also exported crops via river and sea to California when the gold rush created a market for food in the early 1850s and then later to the mining camps of the Northwest. But little could be sent beyond the Pacific coast region until the 1870s because of the expense of hauling bulky commodities long distances. As population densities were low for the most part, markets were small. Most farmers in Sublimity thus raised small quantities of assorted crops, aiming at independence and survival. Their counterparts, further south in the Calapooia Valley, a region of the larger Willamette Valley, also farmed for local production and again only slowly participated in the expanding regional markets that accompanied the gold rush. Farming in the Pacific Northwest was a mixture of the traditional and commercial. The potential for the latter was clearly visible, but was limited. The pattern of the family farm tied to the local community was more dominant (Fite, 1966, pp. 137–55; Gibson, 1985; Boag, 1992, pp. 103–12; May, 1994, pp. 162–84).

In Alpine, pioneer settlers in the 1850s found more problematic environmental conditions for farming and less access to viable transport. As Mormons, they also shared different cultural values, namely finding a haven free from persecution, accepting religious authority and sharing resources. Their early farming ventures were essentially small scale because land was allocated according to family need. Farming was basically subsistence in variety, producing varied crops for family and community consumption. Alpine farmers were not immune to commercial values as some had emigrated from industrial England, but they lacked either adequate or well-endowed land on which to raise surpluses. Indeed in difficult times they might need to seek help from the community storehouse where commodities donated as tithing were held for those in need. This early subsistence farming continued, even when the local rivers and streams were channelled for communal irrigation purposes. Farms then increased somewhat in size, but younger members of families took most of the newly irrigated lands as families tended to stay where they settled. A small number of farmers did produce surpluses in the 1870s for sale in local communities and to transient miners and railroad construction crews. By this time it was apparent that though these Mormons retained a social and religious sense of networking there was no conflict between this sense of community and holding private property. Whenever the land was suitable the Alpine farmers looked to make profits through agriculture and trade. Economic individualism sat side by side with religious solidarity as it did elsewhere in pioneer Utah. This search for agricultural profit would only be consolidated and expanded as railroads increased access to outside markets. (Arrington, 1958, pp. 195–231; May, 1994, pp. 227–43, 258–61; 277–83).

Settlers moving to Middleton, Idaho, during and after the Civil War showed more inclinations to farm commercially as soon as possible. Many had gone west to mine and were imbued with the capitalist ethic. The proximity of mines and boomtowns in the Boise Basin and in Silver City in the Owyhee Mountains enticed pioneers to put more land under cereal cultivation to feed both the miners and the animals which freighted ore and commodities to and from the mines and to provide barley for the local brewing industry. Initially settling in the river valley and then using irrigation to overcome the arid climate, farmers soon started to concentrate on producing one or more cash crops and paid less attention to the crops needed to provide for the family. They continued to produce wheat for miners and hay for draft animals into the 1880s. Their market was essentially local or, at best, regional because of the difficulties of transporting bulky commodities by wagon. Once the Oregon Short Line railroad was completed in 1884 farmers were able to increase their market potential, producing vegetables and fruit in addition to their other crops. They were, however, always limited by the need to irrigate the landscape and by the knowledge that irrigation did not always control the environmental conditions. Farmers in the Boise Valley and in the larger Snake Valley in Idaho in the mid-nineteenth century had commercial aspirations and farmed to cater to these, but they knew that their growing specialist production was hampered by poor transport and could be further hindered by environmental problems (Fite, 1966, pp. 177–8; May, 1994, pp. 35–8, 163–8, 244–58; Fiege, 1999, pp. 17, 37, 120, 145–6, 155–6, 203–9).

Western farming in a national economy

If western agricultural experiences in the mid-nineteenth century offer a variety of aspirations and capacities which demonstrate the coexistence of subsistence economies and commercialism, then their counterparts in the late nineteenth and early twentieth centuries more clearly suggest a much greater propensity for, and commitment to, market involvement. Commercialised farming was increasingly essential to getting by as well as for well-being. However, the gains made from improved technology in the shape of both farm machinery and better access to markets by rails were, for some farmers, offset by the difficulties of belonging to an organised and impersonal national economy and of being part of an international trade network. Add to these considerations the problems arising from environmental adjustments as settlers pushed west into the arid lands and from market adjustments as farmers in older western regions increased competition, then there were many failures and marginal survivors as well as successes. The emphasis certainly shifted towards a Euro-American commercialism as the hallmark of agricultural achievement, but many farmers still operated on a semi-subsistence basis and were closely connected economically as well as socially to their neighbours. The agrarian distress of the 1920s and the 1930s is a testament to the continuance of the struggling family farm.

Transplanted Yankees and farmers from the Old Northwest had already moved into Kansas before the Civil War, but their numbers increased noticeably in the 1870s and 1880s. They were later followed by a variety of European immigrants and second-generation ethnic Americans who moved from areas east of the Mississippi River. The population of Kansas increased rapidly in the post-war years. In the 1870s, despite the depression of mid-decade, it grew by over 630,000 or by 174 per cent. In the 1880s it increased by more than 430,000 or some 44 per cent. The rate of growth then slowed, but continued to expand in absolute numbers as farms filled in and urban centres emerged to service the local economy. Kansas proved to be a popular destination for pioneers because good land was available for settlement free under the 1862 Homestead Act. Several propaganda agencies, such as the State Immigration Bureaus, steamship companies and railroad companies, further stimulated the inflow by advertising the area in glowing terms, thereby portraying visions of a agrarian paradise. The railroads were steadily pushing west, offering transport to markets and improved farm machinery was becoming available as a substitute for family or hired labour. The prospects of making a good living from commercial cereal farming looked promising.

But many would-be Kansas cereal farmers in the decade after the Civil War also knew that in the short term they would have to farm in the older subsistence or semi-subsistence way until they had built up some capital and/or resources, especially if they had to buy land. They thus established small mixed farms in which they raised cereals, hogs and cattle, together with garden and some specialist crops. Little cash outlay was needed if they had migrated with their animals, tools and family for labour. But the margin between success and failure would then be slight. Any natural hazard, for example, hot summers, severe winters, storms, grasshoppers and fires, or a human clash with cattle-drovers and would-be ranchers, could undercut what is best described as a precarious living. Then, too, the market price of cash crops varied, though it fell overall between 1867 and 1897. At the same time, though freight rates on the railroads declined, they were perceived to be too high. The growing impersonal economy offered threats as well as potential as farmers saw themselves caught in a cost-price squeeze. Many succeeded in building up their farms and overcoming natural hazards and market fluctuations. But if resources were meagre then any misfortune could bring ruin. That many succeeded depended on constant hard work and persistence by all members of the family, re-investment of any profit back into the farm, starting out in a period of rising prices and elements of luck. Some settlers migrated to Kansas with more capital and could invest in more land and equipment, but they too were subject to both market forces and natural hazards (Shannon, 1945, pp. 173–96; Fite, 1966, pp. 34–74, Mayhew, 1972).

As Euro-American settlers moved west through eastern Kansas and onto the plains in the late 1870s and 1880s, they faced similar pioneering experiences to those of their counterparts in the western prairies, but they encountered a more hazardous natural environment and a greater personal alienation in the increased commercialism of the agrarian world. The geography of farming produce for external consumption west of the hundredth meridian – the boundary between the sub-humid prairies and the arid plains – namely level topography, absence of trees and insufficient rainfall combined with high winds, made cereal raising, the basis of commercial agrarian farming, at best marginal, at worst ruinous. Though many of these natural conditions had technological solutions in the shape of barbed wire, windmills, irrigation, improved farm machinery, dry farming techniques and crop genetics, these could only be acquired with adequate supplies of capital. The small transplanted American farmer did not have this. He or she depended on gradually building up their farm with profits reinvested from annual sales. But cycles of drought struck western Kansas in the 1880s and 1890s. While the wet years in between encouraged settlement, the droughts brought failure to hundreds of farmers and finally convinced many that they could not use sub-humid farming techniques in the dry lands. They would have to adapt to the environment and for this adaptation they would need to invest in technology. The raising of cereal crops for commercial markets favoured those who either had capital or who had security for credit. It also allowed some immigrants, who knew about farming in dry climates in Europe to use their experience and cultural knowledge to adjust to cycles of rain and drought. But they too had to learn to accommodate to the fluctuations in cereal prices and the rates charged by railroads for storage of crops in elevators and for subsequent transport to central markets (Shannon, 1945, pp. 173–96, 291–309; Fite, 1966, pp. 113–36; Mayhew, 1972; Stratton, 1981, pp. 57–76; Miner, 1986; McQuillan, 1990, pp. 159–89).

Though regional studies within the Plains West provide variations and examine underlying differences in everyday life, agrarian farmers in the region made similar adjustments as those in Kansas. The dry grasslands were indeed fertile if farmed correctly, but the cyclical weather patterns continued. The production of cereal crops here, together with those from other older parts of the west, moved increasingly to the urban markets of North America and into international trade. Farming had for the most part become commercialised and economically impersonal. Those who found difficulties in adjusting to sales in distant markets found some mutual support through farmers' organisations which became active in different parts of the west from the late 1860s. Others gained some assistance from educational agencies whether in the form of farm journals, farm meetings, neighbouring farmers or the agricultural experimental stations and agricultural colleges set up with government assistance (Hurt, 1994, pp. 159–220; Danbom, 1995, pp. 132–60).

Rural communities continued to enjoy a social ethos that sustained individuals in time of need (Riley, 1988, pp. 97–101) if the community as a whole was not undermined by similar distress, but it was very difficult, if not impossible, to survive for long without selling staple crops. This, of necessity, meant commercial farming.

The dry grasslands of the Plains West were not only farmed for cereals; they were also used for raising cattle. This was an extensive rather than intensive form of agriculture and was more suitable to the natural environment. As with cereals, small farmers kept livestock as part of a mixed farm that operated on a subsistence basis. Animals were essential to continued existence and success. They remained valuable working assets until the gasoline-powered tractor began to replace them in the 1920s. They also remained a valuable part of the family's food supply for many years. Pioneer farmers, however, had early learned that they could also sell animals for food to army and fur-trading forts, to transient miners and to railroad construction crews. These were essentially either local or regional markets, but they did point the way to a form of commercialism by establishing the physical possibility of wintering cattle in a cold climate (Osgood, 1929, pp. 1–23).

When the construction of railroads, into and through the western prairies and central plains in the late 1860s and 1870s, opened up the prospects of shipping livestock to urban markets in the Great Lakes region and the northeastern regions, some farmers decided to specialise in raising cattle while others turned to raising corn and hogs. Texas ranchers were already demonstrating the commercial viability of raising cattle. Their herds had multiplied during the Civil War when the advance of the Union troops down the Mississippi River cut off access to any markets other than local. In the late 1860s they experimented with driving their herds north to meet the railroads advancing through Missouri and Kansas. There they could be shipped to Chicago and places to the east. Some of these cattle formed the basis for the expansion of herds on the northern plains. Here livestock grazed freely and safely on the open range, following the domestication of Native Americans in reservations. As overhead costs were low and early profits were high, both American and European capital flowed west, often through formal investment channels (Osgood, 1929, pp. 24–82; Gressley, 1966; Jordan, 1993, pp. 221–36).

Commercial livestock farming expanded and flourished in the northern plains in the late 1870s and early 1880s. This boom, however, was relatively short-lived. The grasslands became over-stocked and the markets became saturated. These environmental and economic problems were compounded by adverse weather conditions in the mid-1880s and by competition for land from cereal farmers. Those who wanted to remain specialist cattle raisers had to adjust to both natural and market conditions. They needed to buy and fence in their land, grow supplementary forage, shelter animals in the winter and use local finance. By systematically organising production to adapt to nature and markets they could make a reasonable living (Osgood, 1929, pp. 83–258; Skaggs, 1986, pp. 50–89; Jordan, 1993, pp. 236–40). But they did not resemble the romantic Hollywood version of cattle ranchers. Nor did their counterparts in older portions of the west. Beef-cattle raisers in Iowa and Illinois, for example, increasingly started to fence in their animals and to fatten them up for market in feedlots. Farmers in Wisconsin turned from raising wheat and running mixed farms to raising dairy cattle to supply the growing needs of the urban population for dairy products (Lampard, 1963; Whitaker, 1975). Whether native-born or of immigrant origin, farmers who wanted to raise livestock became specialised as they aimed for distant commercial markets.

Conclusions

Farming in the American west encompassed a range of adjust-ments, both social and economic. Euro-American settlers responded in a variety of ways to the opportunities presented by selling crops in local, regional, national and international markets. Some pioneers and established settlers with access to capital or credit quickly put higher proportions of their land into cash crops and bought labour-saving machinery when it became available so as to maximise productivity. Their neighbours could be slower to accommodate to commercialism because their farms were smaller or because they were not risk-takers. Alternatively their cultural heritage and their mindset persuaded them that provisioning the family and securing their well-being was their first priority and that they should look to local communal arrangements to establish a rural way of life. Then immigrants and ethnic Americans brought different traditions of farming with them to the west and these they wanted to replicate, at least in part. Add to these considerations the natural hazards and environmental conditions, both of which needed specific responses. The macro approach to examining agricultural history and production has tended to generalise about human responses to creating and developing a farm in the American west, but the social interpretation of living on the land minimises the responses to, and impact of, commercialism and the market economy. Throughout the west there were many types of farmers and there are several ways of passing judgement on their survival and/or success.

5

Making a living:
non-farming occupations

The economy of the American west was not based solely on agriculture. Abundant natural resources provided hunters, trappers, miners and loggers with employment while towns and cities emerged or boomed to support both these businesses and farmers and to offer a range of manufacturing and tertiary occupations. The west was a land of many contrasts among the labour force. There were heroic individualists and anonymous workers. It may be romantic to remember that Buffalo Bill Cody killed many buffaloes when he contracted to supply meat for railroad construction workers in 1867–8; but it may be more realistic to remember that at a similar time Chicago was a major manufacturing and transport centre or that the silver mines of the Comstock Lode were employing hundreds of day labourers in poor conditions. Too much of the workers' history of the west has been written as either adventure stories of the fur traders of the Rocky Mountains, the forty-niners, the cowboys, or the prostitutes with hearts of gold. There were many others in the west who struggled to earn a living through exploiting natural resources or in urban employment. Most were classified as gainfully employed in the census, but there were major differences between the businessmen who did the employing, the workers who were poorly paid and the individuals seeking wealth. All deserve consideration in broadening the assessment of the economic development of the west.

Fur trapping and trading

Native Americans had hunted and trapped for furs long before the Europeans arrived on the North American continent. Animals, ranging in size from the beaver to the bison, were important for both their furs and skins as well as for domestic food and trade with other Native Americans in exchange for corn. Animal skins were used to make clothing, bedding, tools, utensils and many more specific items of material culture. A beaver could supply an acceptable amount of meat for a family while the killing of bison, whether by the whole community or by one hunter could provide some 225 to 550 pounds of meat from each animal (Krech, 1999, pp. 128–35, 179). But for many Native Americans animals were more than sources of survival. They were persons other than humans with whom relationships were social and religious. Native peoples certainly aimed to use and to control nature, but they did this through a form of religious negotiation. They made hunting a sacred ceremony in which some people died so others could live (White, 1994, pp. 237–8). In so doing they wasted some resources, but did not exploit them as heavily as the Europeans for whom animals were commodities with a market and cash exchange value. Then animals were over-hunted by both Native and Euro-Americans, some to the point of extinction.

The European involvement in fur enterprises started when traders and fishermen first landed on the northeast coast in the late fifteenth and early sixteenth centuries. Subsequently, the historical geography of the fur trade spread across the continent. It moved down the St. Lawrence River to and through the Great Lakes, across the Canadian prairies, down the Mississippi River to the Gulf Coast and up the Missouri River long before separate political identities were established in North America. It subsequently featured on the Pacific coast, in the Rocky Mountains and in the Great Plains (Ray, 1996, pp. 54–7, 78–84, 104–6, 102–4, 161–2; Ray, 1998; Hine and Faragher, 2000, pp. 133–58). The French and British in Canada, in the shape of the North West Company and the Hudson's Bay Company crossed boundaries with impunity in the seventeenth, eighteenth and nineteenth centuries and in a similar manner American fur companies were not averse to trapping and trading north of the border. Though companies retained a national identity, they did not worry about the origins of the workers in the field whether they were European, Native American or American; they were more concerned with profits.

The early histories of this international fur trade in the west tended to be company histories or biographies, using whatever archival materials were available. Historians on the Canadian side of the border took advantage of the massive records kept by the Hudson's Bay Company to examine the cautious behaviour of the London-based operation. They also had access to the records of the more flamboyant North West Company whose French and Scottish merchants worked from Montreal. American historians also wrote business histories of major companies or biographies of their owners, such as the Chouteau family of St. Louis, John Jacob Astor and the American Fur Company and Manuel Lisa and the Missouri Fur Company. Such histories were examples of male capitalistic enterprises or case studies of economic relations between the frontier regions and the larger world. As such they were written in terms of the administration of business operations or as an essential part of the lengthy struggle to control the interior of North America (Porter, 1931; Galbraith, 1957; Oglesby, 1963).

Other histories, especially the American ones became adventure stories. Romance flourished when the Euro-American trappers in the Rocky Mountains in the second and third decades of the nineteenth century became 'Mountain Men'. These trappers, who wintered in the mountains and exchanged their beaver catch for several days' worth of drink, gambling and sex, became the heroic figures of many a 'tall tale' and traditional narratives. Masculinity oozed. The picture of the bearded trapper in buckskin leggings and fringed leather jacket contributed to the stereotypical male-dominated west. There was no place for women other than the occasional mention of a 'squaw' in this conquering masculine romp (Billington, R A., 1956, pp. 41–68).

Had historians of the American fur trade crossed the northern border as often as the trappers, they then would have written different histories. They would have benefited from cross-cultural approaches and methodologies at a much earlier stage. For the Canadians were the innovators in fur trade studies in the late 1970s and the 1980s. They displayed a close appreciation of the contributions of Native Americans to the production systems, an increased interest in fur trade society in general and a close analysis of the economics of the fur trade (Wishart, 1992, p. 4; Payne, 2001).

Female historians were important in this revisionism. Educated by feminist studies and equipped with an awareness of multiculturalism, their archival research found that native women were necessary to the success of the fur business. As workers in the business they processed furs and supplied provisions. As sexual partners, they provided family and kin for white traders and helped to create a society of mixed bloods, or Métis, who created a distinctive cultural legacy. As diplomats they negotiated trade relations with First Nations and acted as interpreters. By discussing the role of native women, the face of the Canadian fur trade moved away from the leadership of the company elite or the visions of popular heroes to the previously unknown workers. The centrality of native women also undermined the masculinity of fur trading. Furthermore, it raised issues of race and social hierarchy by examining the relationship between the women who married 'according to the custom of the country' and the incoming white wives of the traders. Tensions at fur-trading posts became an important part of life affecting a range of economic activities (Van Kirk, 1980; Brown, J. S. H. 1980; Peterson and Brown, 1985). Though this centring of women has in turn been criticised, it is now impossible to consider the Canadian fur trade without recognising gendered partnerships and integrating gender considerations of femininity and masculinity into any discussion. Canadian historians also broke new ground in discussing the economic behaviour of both European and native traders. Using the voluminous records of the Hudson's Bay Company they subjected the production figures, trade routes and transport costs of the forts and posts to statistical analysis in order to offer clearer insight into prices paid for furs and the exchange rates for commodities (Ray, 1974, new edn 1998; Ray and Freeman, 1978).

Historians of the American fur trade were slow to follow the gendered social history and the detailed statistical work done by the Canadians some twenty years ago. This delay has stemmed from a variety of reasons. The American fur trade was smaller and lasted a shorter time than its Canadian counterpart and there has not been as much interest in the Métis descendants of native–European unions in the United States. Very few historians of American fur trading were women aware of the trends in women's history. Furthermore, New Western Historians set a different agenda for western history. It remained for historians of the Midwest and the Great Lakes region to rise to the recent challenge of revising American fur trade history. There the French as well as the English were involved in fur trading and they maintained similar patterns of behaviour to those developed north of the border. But Midwestern historians who accepted the findings of Canadian historians found that they could also draw on a different historical tradition. For the New Indian History had already recognised the extensive trade and cultural exchange that took place relatively peacefully between Euro-American incomers and native peoples. They thus both recognised the intercultural contact advocated by American ethnohistorians and followed the Canadian example by giving emphasis to the role of women as cultural mediators and economic partners (White, 1991b; Thorne, 1996; Sleeper-Smith, 2001). Further research on other American fur regions has become more race and gender inclusive, thereby further questioning the dominant masculinity so prevalent in traditional histories (Lansing, 2000).

Though much emphasis has been given to the beaver fur trade, hunting and killing the bison also provided a living for both Native and Euro-Americans. The elimination of the great buffalo herds has recently become a popular topic in environmental as well as fur-trading history. No one knows how many buffaloes there were in pre-contact years. Estimates vary enormously, though figures as high as sixty million have been suggested. However, the native view of vast multitudes throughout much of the continent is a useful approximation and this is supported by the reports of early European invaders (Krech, 1999, pp. 124–6). These multitudes were reduced in many parts of the country, but attention has focused on the grasslands of the Great Plains where most of the animals accumulated. There has been considerable discussion on whether native groups, increasingly mounted on horses, brought to the New World by Europeans and using guns, again a European product, over-hunted the bison as early as 1840 (Flores, 1991; West, 1995, pp. 51–83, Isenberg, 2000, pp. 63–122). Indeed post-revisionist research pushes this date, at least in the southern plains, possibly back to the 1780s or 1790s (Hämäläinen, 2001). But, however early this over-killing started, all recent research on the ecology of the bison has also suggested that natural hazards in the form of drought, fires, wolves, accidents and competition from other grazers, especially horses, together with bovine disease were important considerations. They combined with hunting to produce a volatile natural environment that would deplete the stock of animals. It seems that the supply of buffalo was already at a precarious stage by the mid-nineteenth century.

Though revisionist and post-revisionist researchers have demonstrated that the killing of the bison was a much more complex issue than had earlier been recognised and that over-hunting took place well before the Civil War, no one disputes that the critical crisis occurred during the 1870s and 1880s. Prior to that time, though Native Americans supplied the commercial market in robes as well as hunting bison for subsistence and intertribal trade, the decline was serious but not disastrous. The sale of robes and hides was limited by the quantity that native women could process (Klein, A. M. 1983, pp. 154–5; Wishart, 1992, pp. 92–100). But the continuing ecological pressure on the grasslands of the plains combined with growing commercial pressure for bison products was the *coup-de-grâce*. When the transcontinental railroads were constructed in the 1860s and 1870s, buffaloes were sought as a source of meat supply for the labourers constructing the tracks. Then once opened, the rails gave much easier access to the plains to Euro-American hide-hunters and sportsmen who systematically destroyed the herds. Not only did buffalo tongues become a more widespread delicacy and buffalo hide, complete with hair, become popular, but a new technique for converting hide into commercial leather also made the buffalo a valuable commodity. Moreover, the bones could be ground into fertiliser. Using more powerful rifles, skilled and unskilled hunters and ex-soldiers killed an estimated four to five million animals in three years alone. Such carnage was a year-round business in contrast to the seasonal hunting of the natives in search of buffalo robes. But the native peoples joined in the killing, both for subsistence and commercial purposes. By the 1890s it is estimated that less than 1,000 head of bison remained (Krech, 1999, pp. 140–2; Isenberg, 2000, pp. 123–63). Only in the late twentieth century did the buffalo numbers multiply again.

Fur trading and trapping may not have employed thousands of workers at any given time, even when that activity is extended to include other animals such as deer, muskrat, racoon, fox, mink, sea otter, bear, moose and antelope, but it did contribute in a small way to bringing capital into the west in the early years of Euro-American ownership and occupation. Much more importantly, however, it was of major significance to the livelihood of numerous Native American communities for whom animals were an important source of sustenance and had a religious significance. Furthermore, it should be added that the fur trade did not completely disappear in what might be called the industrial age.

Mining

There were many more miners than fur trappers and traders, least-wise in the American west occupied and owned by Euro-Americans. Most historical attention has been paid to the gold and silver discoveries that markedly changed the early face of California, Nevada and Colorado. Here, and to a lesser extent elsewhere in the west, the individual search for wealth in gold and silver created boom communities. These sometimes developed more mixed economies that in turn stimulated other types of growth. Others faded into insignificance, leaving an environment of ghost towns as well as a debris-strewn and pockmarked landscape. Later discoveries of industrial minerals like coal, copper and iron also stimulated economic growth, often of a dependent or neo-colonial nature as the products were exported out of the west. They also created labouring communities, as increasingly miners became day workers, often on poor pay. Early mining offered glamorous and romantic images of fortunes made, but these faded into the under-side of miners' strikes and mining accidents.

California in 1849 is often considered to be the site of the first western mining rush, though earlier diggings of lead in the Upper Mississippi Valley from the 1820s had triggered a boom, created pockets of population growth and contributed to the growth of St. Louis (Mahoney, 1990, pp. 162–5, 198–202). California can, however, certainly be considered the first large western mining boom and one which had regional and national consequences. These were amply discussed at the time and at the centenary of the gold rush. More recently when the state celebrated the sesquicentennial of its gold rush in 1998 it witnessed another explosion of popular and academic history revisiting and revising its gold rush era experiences (Mann, 1982; Levy, 1992; Rohrbough, 1997; Rawls and Orsi, 1999; Starr and Orsi, 2000). These modern studies have confirmed and extended the economic findings of earlier historians (Paul, 1947) and have substantiated that gold was the cornerstone of California. They have also recast many of the social aspects of pioneer Euro-American California, especially those of gender and race relations. New insights into the human participation in gold rush society and the ecological consequences of mining have raised the profile of ethnic groups and women and have led to criticisms of the wanton destruction of the landscape, but some of these findings have challenged rather than strengthened the interpretations of New Western Historians.

There were many deposits and rich deposits of gold in northern California. Early fortune-seekers were lucky enough to find placer gold eroded from its natural vein and deposited by stream flows near the surface on the foothills of the Sierras. Little skill, equipment or capital was needed to dig for this gold or to separate it from the surrounding gravel. These placer deposits were, however, soon exhausted as the numbers of would-be Argonauts mushroomed from 5,000 in late 1848 to 40,000 a year later and then to 100,000 in 1852. Then miners, whether American or immigrant, responded practically by adapting existing tools and methods to local conditions. They dammed rivers and dug in the riverbeds; they shaped and remoulded hand or foot power to water or steam power and they invented hydraulic mining, or playing a jet of water on a hillside to wash away the earth and provide easier access to the hidden gold-laden gravels. Early hard rock or vein miners found that they could use simple methods if they kept to shallow deposits or if they learned a few basic techniques from more experienced immigrant miners or those from the lead or copper mines in the Great Lakes and Upper Mississippi regions.

But while these miners were adapting to small-scale and often communal enterprises, others became disillusioned. Some returned home. More moved elsewhere in the Far West and Mountain West in search of gold or silver or they stayed in California and changed occupation. Yet other miners had to face the realities of the industrial age and become labourers in lode mines (Mann, 1982, pp. 29–51). Gold continued to be found in deep veins in California throughout much of the late nineteenth century, but mining then required knowledge of geology and complex technology. Larger companies were formed in the 1860s and 1870s to acquire the capital and machinery and to develop the organisation to extract gold at depth. Mining had reached industrial status with financial investors operating through the stock markets, engineers and super-intendents using professional and managerial skills, owners living in San Francisco and waged labour working deep underground (Paul, 1947; Rohrbough, 1997, pp. 119–41, 185–215; Limbaugh, 1999; Cornford, 1999).

Gold had been the magnet attracting migrants to California in the late 1840s and early 1850s and for a short time it provided many thousands with an occupation. But even before the placer deposits became more difficult to locate, some miners decided that they could earn a better living by providing services for the Argonauts. Here, distance from other settled parts of the United States and the rapid growth of population without developing a parallel infrastruc-ture meant an absence or paucity of such commodities as food, clothing and shelter and of such services as lawyers, doctors, restaurants, laundries, tailors or entertainers. Though the Spanish and Mexican antecedent residents could offer some provisions, some miners who had found little gold took up farming or moved into commerce and manufacturing. Those with previous profes-sional experience taught in schools, ran newspapers or opened a law office. The continued mining of gold, the temperate climate and the proximity of the Pacific coast, which facilitated a thriving maritime trade, provided the impetus for the gold rush boom to stimulate a more stable and balanced economy. But equally, if not more important, California, and San Francisco in particular, became the provisioning centre for other inland mining strikes in the 1850s and 1860s. By the time that the transcontinental railroads tied the Pacific coast to mainstream America, northern California had a broad economic base.

Other centres of mining for gold and silver in the Pacific West and Mountain West were not as fortunate as northern California in the wealth and nature of their precious minerals and the attractiveness of their location. Strikes in the Fraser River, British Columbia, in 1858, in eastern Oregon, Montana and Idaho in the 1860s, in the Black Hills of Dakota and in Tombstone, Arizona, in the mid-1870s, in the Coeur d'Alene region in Idaho in 1883 and then in the Klondike in Canada in 1898 and in Nome, Alaska, in 1900, created pockets of temporary settlement for the duration of relatively easy placer mining. Only if quartz mining followed with capital and technology as it did in the Coeur d'Alene region did large-scale industrial mining follow. Then miners became labourers working for wages in a dangerous environment and living in grim isolated communities (Paul, 1963, pp. 37–55, 135–60, 178–96; Schwantes, 1996, pp. 212–15). They had joined the workforce of industrial America.

Colorado and Nevada were the sites of two major rushes that offered industrial labour and living prospects earlier in the nineteenth century. Of the thousands who initially migrated to Colorado in 1859 mainly from the Mississippi and Ohio Valleys, many did not stay long. Early mining focused on placer deposits along or near streams and these were soon exhausted. Lode gold was buried in sulphur-rich rocks, but this required both technology for processing and capital for investment. These were not forthcoming until the end of the troubled 1860s when both gold and silver production expanded rapidly. Better access to markets through new mountain roads and then rails facilitated growth but the local economy was subject to slumps because of collapsing silver markets. Only the rising demand for base metals like zinc and lead which were abundant in Colorado's silver districts, helped revive the area. Even then the expansion was cyclical because it was linked to world markets (Paul, 1963, pp. 109–34; Bryant, 1994, pp. 202–3; Wyckoff, 1999, pp. 25–60, 73–8).

As in Colorado, early mineral finds in Nevada were short-lived. Isolated placer diggings gave way to quartz mining when the Comstock Lode was discovered in 1859. But to reach the deeply located gold and silver safely, owners had to import and adapt technology from many parts of the world and to acquire enough capital for large-scale operations. Crushing machinery driven by steam power was required to release the minerals which then needed to be smelted. Mining required drilling and blasting and the mines needed heavy timbering to prevent cave-ins and pumps to protect from flooding. Skilled miners, often from abroad, as well as unskilled men were employed and the number of workers rose from some 1,500 in the 1860s to over 3,000 in the 1870s. Freighting over the mountains, lumbering and the mercantile trade importing food and commodities from both Utah and California became profitable ventures for those with some capital. But it all collapsed when the precious metals ran out and Virginia City, an urban centre whose population may have reached 25,000 in the mid-1870s, became a virtual ghost town in the 1890s (Paul, 1963, pp. 56–108; Bryant, 1994, pp. 200–1).

There was a boom and slump pattern of economic and urban growth associated with mining and subsidiary activities in many parts of the Mountain and Far Wests. This was linked to resource exploitation and industrial capitalism in that there was a wealth-seeking capacity to develop minerals. Though gold and silver were precious minerals that could buy instant gratification, and may be readily explicable in terms of exploitation, this was not the same for such base minerals as lead and copper. Nevertheless they too were quickly used, as was coal when it was discovered. By the 1860s and 1870s the demands of not only industrialising America but also the global economy put pressure on companies, increasingly using investment funds and requiring expensive technology, to seek rapid profits. The mining west was not part of a pattern of agrarian expansion. It was in the words of William Robbins, 'the paradox of the machine in the garden' (Robbins, 1994, pp. 83–102).

Mining left a legacy of unstable communities with high social and environmental costs. In human terms mining meant using cheap labour. For deep mining, skilled engineers and miners were required, but there were many tasks that could be accomplished by cheap unskilled labour, especially if foreign-born. Early placer deposits attracted ordinary people because no experience or training was required to dig for either gold or silver and no special equipment was needed. In hard rock mining, however, where it was necessary to dig tunnels, use dynamite, separate the mineral from the quartz and smelt metal, not only those with skills but also menial workers were required. The growth of day or weekly labourers created insecurity. Itinerant miners were, for many years in the late-nineteenth century, the largest non-agricultural work force in the Trans-Missouri West. Frequently young, single, ethnic and racial, these men faced hard, dangerous and monotonous work in the bowels of the earth. Some, along with their married co-workers, became involved in strikes and unions to improve their conditions.

The radical Western Federation of Miners, formed in 1893, combined local groups in an attempt to stop the use of the military against workers. Soon it had over 50,000 members in the west. Other miners, both single and married, remained quiescent or willing to work their way quietly to greater security (Wyman, 1979; Schwantes, 1987; Schwantes, 1994, pp. 437–45; Bryant, 1994, pp. 197–208; Jameson, 1998). Though many minority workers faced prejudice and discrimination, some ethnic labourers saw mining as a chance to improve their lot. They managed to build viable and relatively successful lives in their mining communities (Zhu, 1997).

Environmental damage from mining was long lasting. Contemporaries and modern visitors alike have easily identified mining sites from the scarred landscape. Mining of all kinds altered vegetation, with hydraulic mining bringing wholesale destruction. In many parts of the west mining requirements quickly destroyed local supplies of timber and more had to be imported from within the region. Surfaces and materials were removed altering landscapes and again hydraulic mining brought massive changes. In California where it had its major impact, it left massive holes in hillsides, with tailings forming huge dumps. It also diverted streams and changed the character of rivers. Dredges, though used less extensively, also piled up mounds of gravel in the form of ridges. Lode mining impacted on smaller areas than placer mining and took place underground, but nevertheless it disfigured the environment with mine dumps. But more noticeable at the time and visible in the photographs was the air pollution caused by milling and smelting and the water pollution created by dumping. Add to the devastation of nature, the constructed debris of shacks and lean-tos, mills, machinery and ghost towns, and the mining legacy can only be called negative. Mining helped to create a fragile environment as well as an economy with irregular growth potential (Rohe, 1986, 1995; Smith, D. A. 1993, pp. 1–24; Dasmann, 1999, pp. 116–20; Smith, D. A. 1999).

Forestry

Forestry or lumbering also created long-lasting legacies. Whether located in the Great Lakes region or in the Pacific Northwest, the growth of lumbering was tied into regional and global markets and followed a boom and slump pattern. Its face was ugly, both in terms of human and environmental qualities. Small-scale saw mills operating on a local level and often in the early years of settlement could make competencies. But aggressive entrepreneurs who speculated in large tracts of timber dominated the industry. They employed hundreds of wage labourers who used an increasingly sophisticated cut and slash technology to plunder resources (Robbins, 1994, pp. 128–9). These loggers and mill workers struggled to make their living in hard and challenging situations in which they were vulnerable to economic forces beyond their control and faced many industrial hazards. The end product of their activity, processed wood and wood products, was certainly a leading industry throughout much of the nineteenth century, but the exploitation of lumber bequeathed massive debris, which was only partially offset by conservationists' efforts to replant.

Early lumbering in northern New England and the western parts of New York and Pennsylvania, served the needs of regional farmers, urban centres, shipbuilding and allied industries. By the 1830s, however, these extensive forests had been denuded. Increasingly timber speculators and loggers looked to the pineries of the Great Lakes for their living. Here, towering strands of virgin white pine and hardwood covered northern Michigan, Wisconsin and Minnesota and gradually tapered off in a northwesterly direction into western Canada. These rich resources were first explored and 'cut into' on a piecemeal basis in the 1830s and 1840s and then more systematically in the following three decades. Initially there was a local and regional demand for wood from both farmers and the growing lake and river cities. But the location of these forests in close proximity to the water transport of the Great Lakes, the Erie Canal and the Mississippi River and its tributaries enabled lumbermen to reach more distant markets with their bulky low-value commodities.

Aided by improving technology, including the application of steam power, the use of circular saws, which facilitated continuous fast cutting and labour-saving devices like the endless chain device to speed up the feeding stage of bringing logs to mills, Midwestern lumbering became more systematic in the 1860s and 1870s. Increasingly corporations rather than companies sold lumber in emerging national markets. They supported the construction of railroads into pine-producing areas, not only to open up new resources, but also to improve their access to markets. Mills grew larger and more elaborate and lumber towns sprang up and then disappeared as timber was 'cut over'. Though lumber production continued to increase until the early 1890s, entrepreneurs were already looking ahead for new reserves in the 1870s. They knew that their assault on the forests had a limited lifespan and that they would need to move on if they were to continue making profits (Fries, 1951; Walsh, 1972, pp. 98–140; Williams, 1989, pp. 193–237; Cronon, 1991, pp. 148–206).

Some lumbermen looked south to the yellow pine areas of the Gulf States. Others looked west to the pine and redwood forests of the Pacific and Mountain regions where they ran into competition with firms already established by New England and California finance. These early tidewater operators in the Northwest and California had cut timber from the public domain for sale to the California mines. Seeing a regional market in the emerging towns and mines and a potential export market overseas using San Francisco as a transhipment point, they invested more capital in purchasing lands and in the construction of short railroads to supplement the waterways to their mills. They further expanded by bringing in new equipment and experienced workers to speed up the processing of logs. Their successes attracted the attention of Midwesterners looking for new resources in which they could invest their own capital and funds from the stock market (Williams 1989, pp. 291–5; Bryant, 1994, pp. 225–6).

These new firms competed with established west-coast lumbermen for large tracts of forests. Using more sophisticated technology driven by steam power and shipping wood and wood products by rail to the interior markets of North America rather than the more irregular coastal markets, they built giant integrated enterprises. These businesses were manned by young, single and frequently immigrant workers who lived in wretched conditions in lumber camps, laboured long hours in difficult conditions and faced dangerous tasks cutting trees, damming streams, rafting logs to mills and then processing them. The pressure of work was fast and the industrial accident rate was high. Profits were also potentially high as capitalists harvested timber rapidly. There was little incentive to conserve, because lumber was abundant. It was easy to cut only the best strands and move on. Indeed the rate of expansion accelerated in the early twentieth century when a group of Great Lakes lumbermen and businessmen, headed by the tycoon Frederick Weyerhauser, bought a huge tract of prime forest land from the Northern Pacific Railway Company and then added more holdings. Aiming to control the industry and hopefully to stabilise prices and outputs, the new venturers only succeeded in further contributing to overproduction. Lumber mills in the Northwest and California, like mines, produced more than could be consumed locally. National and international markets thus played a major role in the economic health of the region and were often responsible for its instability (Robbins, 1988, pp. 22–67, 1997, pp. 210–21; Williams, 1989, pp. 296–330; Schwantes, 1996, pp. 215–22). Economically the western lumber industry was volatile.

It was not, however, irreplaceable. Unlike minerals it was possible to replenish tree stocks. The assaults of lumber tycoons in the Lakes after the Civil War and in the Pacific and Mountain Wests from the 1880s rang warning bells, not merely among intellectuals and journalists, but among scientists, government officials and even a handful of men in the industry. Civil servants knew that lumbermen and speculators were abusing the land laws to obtain timberlands free or cheaply and were cutting trees both illegally and inefficiently. Early efforts to rectify exploitation and fraud for the most part fell on deaf ears. Pressure groups like the 'wilderness is beautiful' Sierra Club (1892), professional organisations like the American Forestry Association (1875) and journals like *Garden and Forest* (1888–97), which spread information on forestry topics, started to raise some awareness. They created an emotional and moral response to perceived abuses. By itself this growing consciousness was inadequate to make progress. It needed the federal government, increasingly persuaded by arguments about resource management, to make some headway with setting aside forest reserves and with planning to rehabilitate denuded areas. The battle for forest conservation was by no means won, even with over 150 million acres of land in forest reserves by 1906, a revitalised forest service formally acknowledged in the shape of the United States Forest Service in 1905 and a president, Theodore Roosevelt (1901–9), committed to environmentalism. There were considerable differences between members of the various departments involved in conservation. Furthermore, the mindset of plunder remained strong and political in-fighting between western and eastern groups as well as opposition to increased government intervention prevented any large-scale constructive help for the environment. Nevertheless a foundation had been laid for the management of forests to sustain a high yield and to provide a continuous supply of timber (Hays, 1959; Gates, 1968, pp. 531–606; Robbins, 1985, pp. 1–33; Williams, 1989, pp. 393–424; Cronon, 1994, pp. 607–11; Pisani, 1996, pp. 119–58).

Manufacturing

The growth of primary activities in both the farming and non-agricultural sectors of the western economy in turn stimulated local manufacturing. Processing industries early disseminated an industrial experience to the newly settling country. They provided some of the necessities of life in the early west, like wood, wooden products and flour. Moreover, they added value to local materials, thereby stimulating capital investment and offering work, frequently in towns and cities. Other industries also emerged to service the daily needs of new settlers and long-term residents. It was possible to import such household and commercial goods from older and better-established firms in the northeastern region. But the price of shipping such goods and waiting for replies encouraged many entrepreneurs to set up business in the west to cater to increased western population. There were many opportunities to make a living in western industry and these grew. The continuing settlement of the west into the early twentieth century certainly enhanced the productive capacity of the economy while rising levels of productivity, consequent on technological improvements, facilitated the development of the manufacturing sector, especially in the Midwest and Far West.

The processing branches were the leading sectors of industrialisation in the west. Taking advantage of rich forest resources, varied mineral deposits and increasing agricultural outputs from commercial farmers, numerous mill- and craft-shop owners initially supplied the needs of local communities for lumber, flour, iron products, small machinery, clothing and domestic utensils. But these small artisan-style entrepreneurs were rapidly overtaken by merchants who quickly realised the potential of moving into processing. As these newly-fledged western manufacturers expanded their capital and their markets, they were assisted or outmanoeuvred by eastern businessmen who either invested in the established processing industries or came west themselves to establish their own industrial enterprises. The rapid spread of railroads throughout the west from the 1850s weakened the position of processors in small scattered towns and in some cities that had benefited from water transport. But processing forged ahead in many cities and after the Civil War economies of scale and internal reorganisation within firms assured the rise of large enterprises that took a leading position not only in the west, but also in the nation.

Meat packing demonstrates how the processing industry developed in the west in the years up to the 1920s. In the early years of settlement it was a small and scattered mercantile activity, located on or near waterways for transport to markets. The growth of railroads and the technology of refrigeration changed the shape and structure of the industry. Good rail connections both for receiving western livestock and for dispatching meat products more rapidly to urban markets encouraged the concentration of the industry, initially in Chicago and other large cities like St. Louis and Milwaukee, but also later in Kansas City. Ice packing and the use of the refrigerated railroad car by 1880 facilitated year-round processing and promoted the chilled beef and pork business at the expense of the barrelled salted-pork trade. Internal administrative reforms and changes in marketing and distribution then consolidated the growth of big firms such that the business became oligopolistic. Progressive reform brought a degree of regulation of meat products, but little change in the structure of the industry. The industry was a western activity and remained primarily a western activity providing a living for many hundreds of workers (Yeager, 1981; Walsh, 1982, 2003; Cronon, 1991, pp. 207–59).

Processing agricultural products may have been more developed in the Midwest because of access to supply and because of the early development of industries. But it was by no means alone. Lumber processing flourished in the Upper Mississippi Valley from the late 1850s and on the Pacific coast from the 1870s. In northern Wisconsin, for example, a series of mill towns emerged in the

1850s in the Wolf River region north of Lake Winnebago. Lumbering continued to flourish into the 1890s because of the proximity to lumber supplies and the construction of railroads. Further west, the greater accessibility to forests by rail and the supply of capital by lumber tycoons and and smaller investors through the stock market led to the creation of such manufacturing towns as Everett on the Puget Sound and the integrated operations of Coos Bay in southern Oregon (Walsh, 1972, pp. 106–11; Robbins, 1988, pp. 26–53; Williams, 1989, pp. 214, 216).

Smelting, or processing ores into a fluid state was an essential stage in separating minerals from their encasing materials. Smelters were located near to mining operations in a considerable number of western cities. They processed gold, silver, lead and copper, belching out acrid fumes. For example, in Montana, copper smelting developed in both Butte and in nearby Anaconda. These industries created poor working conditions and clouds of pollution, but they lured men from nearby rural areas and offered employment to thousands. Smelting became a significant manufacturing enterprise in several mountain states (Paul, 1963, pp. 102, 103–5, 119–20, 123–4, 128–30, 150–5; Mercier, 2001, pp. 30–5).

Processing may well have been the industrial activity most suited to the economy of the west, but it was not the only branch of manufacturing. Heavy industries were economically viable as local demands for farm machinery, steam engines, mill and rail equipment increased. Early western iron founders and merchants could supply this demand because they were protected from the competition of larger established firms in the east by the difficulties of shipping heavy goods long distance. When the decline in freight rates gradually resolved this problem from the 1850s, some western businesses had accumulated sufficient capital, technological knowledge and reputation to withstand eastern competition and to search out new markets for themselves in more recently settled areas. Farm machinery manufacturer Cyrus Hall McCormick, who moved west in 1847, initially sold his reapers to customers in the nearby Chicago hinterland. Technical improvements to the reaper, advertisements about the value and nature of the machine and the use of agents to demonstrate, repair and arrange credit for the machine introduced the machine to farmers while the railroads distributed it to a much larger area. McCormick and some of his smaller competitors like

J. I. Case of Racine, Wisconsin, built up strong enterprises that were sufficiently innovative to make such contacts (Walsh, 1972, pp. 148–56; Hounshell, 1984, pp. 152–87). As economies of scale improved efficiency in larger and increasingly national operations, some western establishments found they were unable to compete and either concentrated on local sales, shut down or were amalgamated.

Similar trends were visible in manufacturing enterprises producing domestic consumer goods for sale in local markets. In the years before 1870 artisans such as tailors, dressmakers, milliners, shoemakers and cabinetmakers were able to make a living by producing bespoke articles (Riley, 1988, pp. 109–10, 129–30). Their trade was protected by a semi-isolated western market and was not yet threatened by imports of cheaper batch or mass-produced commodities manufactured by machinery and division of labour. But such shelter was potentially vulnerable to imports of cheap manufactures shipped west at relatively low cost either by water or later by rail. Although some western entrepreneurs planned to invest capital into converting their shops into factories, employing technology and unskilled labour, many found that they could not withstand the competition of larger eastern factories employing economies of scale in the late nineteenth century. They were now part of a national market. Certainly western companies continued to produce household and personal goods, but they were increasingly challenged by the cost and style of products from older parts of the country as railroads accelerated transport and reduced freight costs.

Merchants had imported consumer goods to burgeoning urban centres like Cincinnati, Chicago and San Francisco before the advent of rails, but the range and quantity of their commodities varied considerably with access to waterways, distance from east-coast cities, season of the year and their personal credit rating. Initially they solicited custom by listing their imported merchandise in the local newspapers as stocks arrived. As they built up trade they were able to offer a variety of services, but many preferred to keep their dry goods or general provisions trade. They knew that there would always be a demand for such goods as cloth, domestic utensils, hardware and groceries and that they could make their living as retailers if they could establish their reputation and acquire the cash and credit to purchase more merchandise. Those who became more specialised moved into trade in regional produce like lead, wheat or livestock. They shipped such produce out of the region. Others took on wholesaling as well as retailing functions and sold manufactured goods to merchants in smaller towns. These merchants, in turn, often undertook a dual function of buying farm produce from their rural customers and selling them groceries, dry goods and hardware in exchange. There was a regional urban system moving currents of trade in the early west and employing a multitude of merchants. Much further west in gold-rush San Francisco, merchants imported nearly everything from food and clothing to building materials and mining equipment because of its port status and distance from other communities. Indeed merchants were among the Californians who made their fortunes because they were intermediaries retailing scarce commodities in years in which money or gold was available (Atherton, 1939; Paul, 1963, pp. 48–51; Pomeroy, 1965, pp. 121–4; Abbot, 1981, pp. 41–108; Mahoney, 1990, pp. 89–272; Cronon, 1991, pp. 318–24).

This mercantile network changed with the advent and improvement of railroads and with the consequent development of a national economy. Town merchants could travel more rapidly and more frequently to a regional wholesale centre and could purchase a larger variety of goods in smaller quantities. They neither needed as much storage space as formerly, nor as much capital. And they looked more often to the rising cities of the west than those of the east for their supplies. Merchants from the Upper Mississippi River valley towns strengthened their ties with the metropolitan city of Chicago, but it was also possible for merchants in Kansas and Nebraska to purchase and sell Chicago goods. Still further west, merchants in the diverse mining settlements of Colorado were supplied from Chicago by rail and then by freighting companies. Only when Denver emerged as a regional gateway in the 1870s and 1880s did wholesaling houses there take a more active economic role in the mountain region. On the Pacific coast, San Francisco rapidly became the mercantile gateway with its commercial hinterland stretching inland through the mountain region, up and down the coast and across the Pacific Ocean. As it had developed a manufacturing profile during the 1860s and 1870s, so its merchants distributed local as well as imported products to a widespread hinterland (Pomeroy, 1965, pp. 124–8; Hogan, 1990, pp. 19–48;

Cronon, 1991, pp. 324–33; O'Connor, 1994, pp. 541–5; Wyckoff, 1999, pp. 108–112). Merchants were essential to the well-being of the western economy.

The traditional perception of the western economy in the years before the First World War has been that of a resource-rich area containing an abundance of minerals and lumber in the Mountain West and Far West and good farmland in the Plains and Midwest. Many residents made their living working with these resources. But they were not alone. There was also an industrial and commercial west which was located in cities, required many wageworkers and investment of capital and was tied to a fluctuating world economy. Processing industries, the production of machinery and equipment, whether for farming or mining, and the manufacture of some consumer goods together with an extensive export and import trade to, from, and within, the west were of major importance to economic well-being. This development of manufacturing and trade in turn stimulated the formation of a service sector. Urban workers ranged from shopkeepers, domestic employees, cooks and laundry personnel to teachers, bankers, lawyers and journalists. Both cities and farms grew simultaneously in the American west into the early years of the twentieth century (Nugent, 2001, pp. 131–3).

6
Western communities

The American west was composed of diverse communities. There was no distinctive or uniform model, such as hypothesised by Frederick Jackson Turner in 1893. Migrants' confrontation with nature did not strip them of their cultural inheritance and produce new people and societies of a specifically western character or with other distinctive traits. Migrants retained many of their traditional values and adapted many of their institutions at the same time as adjusting to the natural environment and adopting some of the manners and mores of whoever was in authority. The result was a proliferation of small communities that existed like island archipelagos, sometimes coexisting within a defined geographical space, yet distinctly separate.

These western communities had porous boundaries and were both geographically and chronologically transient. Some merged into each other for geographical reasons, as when immigrants moved to a new area or an already settled area and accommodated to their neighbours' economic lifestyles, if not their cultural values. Others changed gradually over time as newcomers adjusted both to their natural and socio-cultural environments and took advantages of changes in technology. The communities were both rural and urban, immigrant and native, religious and secular, voluntary and organised.

Drawing a snapshot picture at any given point in time does not reflect how many differences existed. More appropriate both to actual experiences and to recent historical concerns to reflect multiplicity and complexity is a depiction of small clusters of family and friends, ethnic communities, organised bodies and economic interest groups. Their common denominator was shared experiences, but this sharing cannot be made into a universal experience (White 1991a, pp. 298–327; Hine and Faragher, 2000, pp. 362–400). Moving both through space and time it is possible to capture a flavour of the adjustments and retentions that have made the American west such a challenging area to interpret. Above all, however, is the acceptance of diversity as a basic tool for the modern understanding of the human composition of the west.

Native Americans at contact

Sioux migrations from the Upper Mississippi Valley and their diverse settlements in the plains point to the complexity of community creation within what has been perceived to be a common Native American language group. At contact (1492), the Sioux were not a single community, though they spoke related dialects. The Siouan family included, among others, the Winnebago, the Santee, the Tetons, the Hunkpapa, the Oglala and the Mandans. Collectively they lived in parts of the Mississippi and Missouri River Valleys where they had been pushed from their earlier homes in the Ohio River Valley by the expansion of the Iroquois and Algonquin. In their new territory they adjusted their lifestyles from their previous farming existence. The Teton (Lakota) Sioux moved west of the Missouri River in South Dakota, dominating that area as nomadic hunters once they had acquired horses. The Santee in the northlands of Minnesota followed a mixed economy, raising crops, hunting, fishing and gathering rice in the rivers and many lakes of the area. The Mandans on the fertile lands of the upper Missouri River and its tributaries in North Dakota, combined farming crops with gathering wild plants and hunting buffalo (Gibson, A. M. 1980, pp. 69–71; Sturtevant, 2001, pp. 94, 102–3, 349, 351, 761, 762, 794).

In 1492 the Mandans lived in large semi-permanent villages. Their houses were either the tipi variety built round centre poles and covered with hides supported by frameworks of cottonwood and willow or circular, dome-shaped earth lodges. These were constructed closely together to offer shelter from the elements of heat, cold and the perennial wind and also as a fortification to protect themselves and their food caches. Their subsistence economy was based on a gender division of labour in which the men hunted and the women farmed. Men hunted buffalo on foot in large groups in order to drive the animals over cliffs or trap them in corrals. The community then used the carcasses for food, clothing, shelter and tools. Women raised corn, squash and sunflowers in the soft soils of the river flood plains. They needed considerable skill and knowledge to raise ample food in the short growing seasons of the northern plains and to harvest and process their crops with such primitive tools as digging sticks, bone hoes and horn rakes. The older men raised tobacco for their own use. Religion was an essential ingredient in this way of life and the Mandans surrounded themselves with ceremonies and rituals to ask for successful hunting, good harvests and the well-being of the community. They knew that their existence was precarious. In good seasons they were well supplied. But as they lived close to nature they did sometimes need to trade for meat and hides and could be threatened by raids on their normally ample food supplies. Theirs was an existence that European incomers found difficult to comprehend (Lowie, 1954, pp. 21–5, 31–8; Hurt, 1987, pp. 58–62; Iverson, 1992, pp. 89–93, Carlson, 1998, pp. 42, 51–66, 115).

Reservation communities

Americans and Euro-Americans continued to experience problems in understanding Native American communities other than as reformulated according to their own individualistic and enterprising value system. Having pushed diverse native communities westward, or onto smaller plots of their former homelands since the founding of the nation, and then, having exhausted what was considered valuable land, most welcomed official government policy that confined different communities to reservations. In these restricted spaces in the post-Civil War years Native Americans met assimilation head-on as they were required to adapt to Euro-American modes of living. Often unable and unwilling to adjust they made some accommodations, but they overtly and subtly resisted many attempts to undermine their culture and their customs.

Community life on reservations was miserable and demoralising. Federal officials insisted that male heads of households farm, even though there was little tradition of individual enterprise and often the land was unsuitable or difficult to work. Genuine efforts were frustrated because of defective tools and poor seeds and would-be farmers also faced the natural hazards of the weather and insects. Many families soon became dependent on inadequate supplies and rations provided by the federal government. Subsequently these could be withheld from those whom the Indian agent perceived to be reluctant to work. Achieving economic livelihood on the reservations was difficult.

Maintaining traditional cultural patterns was also very tricky. Civilisers aimed to create a new social order. Teachers in both the reservation schools and the distant boarding schools preferred mechanical and agricultural subjects for the boys and cooking, sewing and laundry work for girls. Such subjects supposedly equipped young native people for Euro-American style life, even though this life was rarely viable on the reservations. Missionaries attempted to introduce a Christian version of civilisation to reservation residents. Native Americans, however, found that some of the basic concepts like penance and baptism were alien and preferred to retain their own religious ceremonies, often in secret. Alternatively they indigenised Christianity. They also retained their own legal system despite the introduction of native police. Conflict was frequent as white Americans attempted to civilise the native and failed. Some went along half-heartedly as a means of getting rations; others continued to retain elements of their former mores. Life in the contact-period plains may have been hard, but it was open. Life on the reservations was grim and subservient (Hoxie, 1984; Wishart, 1994, pp. 141–8; Carlson, 1998, pp. 163–82; Utley, 2003, pp. 219–41).

Minority communities

Though Native Americans were distinctive in the American west because they resided on the land prior to European contact, they have been treated as a minority group alongside more recent arrivals. Minority here, however, refers to racial or racial-ethnic labelling by incomers and the language used in this context can become very intricate and sensitive. Americans of different backgrounds have regularly redefined race and ethnicity in their relationships with one another. In the nineteenth and early twentieth centuries the dominant white cultural group, Anglo-Saxon Protestants, often identified European immigrants as Black, or 'Dagoes' rather than as Irish, German or Italian. Only gradually did such immigrants lose their specific ethnicity and become white as they merged into a larger fluid group called Euro-American. This whiteness then collapsed substantial differences of ethnic culture, religion, class and historical experience into one category that often excluded 'others'. In recent times of multicultural awareness, these 'others' identified by the colour of their skin and by their race, regardless of the many differences within each group, have been labelled minorities. This naming can have a double sense of being numerically smaller and being perceived as inferior to Euro-Americans. It has also become a means of trying to ensure that groups that have suffered from discrimination and have been hidden from or marginal to history are brought into the centre (Roediger 1994a; Jameson and Armitage, 1997, pp. 5–9; Frankenberg, 1997a; Jacobsen, 1998, pp. 1–14).

Both African-Americans and Chinese immigrants were minorities who adapted to an American west dominated by Euro-Americans and their institutions. The former were as much native-born as were white Americans, but the Chinese in the nineteenth century remained aliens and were treated as such. African-Americans migrated westward across the southern sections of the United States as both slaves and free persons. They were an essential part of the process of western agricultural settlement, for without their labour little cotton would have been raised until the early twentieth century when mechanisation was introduced. Much western history however, even prior to the establishment of the west as a region by New Western Historians, has been written excluding the region of the south. Research on African-Americans has thus focused on either the sectional struggle about the extension of slavery into the west and its political repercussions or on black individuals or small black communities who migrated to a variety of western areas seeking to avoid segregation and discrimination and to find better opportunities of making a living (Billington, M. and Hardaway, 1998; Taylor, 1998; Taylor and Wilson Moore, 2003).

Two African communities in the west have received considerable attention, the Buffalo Soldiers and the migrants to Kansas in the late 1870s. The 25,000 African-Americans who served in four regiments between 1866 and 1917 have caused considerable controversy. In being recognised as a specific group in the federal army in the west they gained reluctant acceptance and some authority. But in being part of an army that fought and restrained Native Americans and striking workers, they have been perceived to be working against racial minorities and their own social class (Taylor, 1998, pp. 164–91). The Exodusters have been treated more sympathetically. When there was little or no land reform in the post-Civil War south some free black Americans looked to the west, and in particular to Kansas, to improve their circumstances. Following the establishment of an agrarian community in western Kansas in 1875 and the circulation of information about Kansas some three years later, more black settlers headed north. Perhaps 20,000 migrants joined the black 'rush' to Kansas in 1879–80. Though some remained to farm the dry lands of western Kansas or in all-black communities, others moved into the earlier settled Kansan towns and formed separate neighbourhoods (Painter, 1971; White, 1991a, pp. 197–9; Taylor, 1998, pp. 36–43; Hine and Faragher, 2000, pp. 370–3).

Yet more African-Americans were scattered in discrete small enclaves within white or Euro-American communities. Here they faced discrimination in jobs, housing and social relations, but they remained free agents and their local environment, though not supportive, was generally non-threatening. On the whole African-Americans felt more positive about life in the west than in the south in that their relative scarcity in numbers posed no threat to the surrounding Euro-Americans. They entered a range of activities. There were female and male African-Americans, sometimes slave, more often free, among the early explorers and the fur trappers in the Rocky Mountains. They were also in the army, farmed, homesteaded and drove cattle, mined and worked in a variety of occupations in all black towns and as unskilled labour in black ghettoes within large white communities. As such workers black Americans had limited agency and bargaining power. They were more successful in establishing their own social institutions, like churches, fraternal organisations, newspapers and clubs. Though never accepted as equals, African-Americans in the west gained the ability to live their lives within black communities and were able to build a small amount of economic independence, especially when catering to all black communities. Historians are increasingly locating these communities, however small, and are thereby painting the west in a darker hue (Billington and Hardaway, 1998; Taylor, 1998; De Leon, 2002).

Chinese-Americans were also locked into segregated units, whether as workers or as residents. Arriving on the west coast of northern California at the time of the gold rush, the predominantly male immigrants found that despite their willingness to work hard and their desire to cause no trouble, they were regarded as aliens and aroused deep racial hatred. This hostility was both economic and cultural. As workers, Chinese males were industrious, but they laboured in a two-tiered system in which they were always relegated to arduous, unskilled and low-paid jobs (White, 1991a, pp. 282–4). In mining, they worked on exhausted claims and less profitable diggings both in California and the Mountain West. Even so, they were accused of taking profits out of the country and were targeted by the Alien Tax of 1852. As labourers they were a major force in constructing the Central Pacific Railroad through the Sierra Mountains. Again they were disliked and hired only because of their diligence and cheap labour. They were further valued as migrant farm workers until intimidated by white vigilantes. In the towns, Chinese took jobs that were normally done by women, running restaurants and laundries and catering to the needs of their own male-dominant communities by operating shops, gambling and opium dens and brothels (Paul, 1988, pp. 158–63; Takaki, 1989, pp. 80–94; Tong, 2003, pp. 36–43). Of the few Chinese women who went to California many were prostitutes and their lives were much worse than those of males (Yung, 1995, pp. 26–34). If jealousy over hard work was not enough to arouse white racists, then the arrival of many Chinese on the ticket system, whereby they worked off payment for their passage, meant they were frequently viewed as despised peon labourers.

Culturally the Chinese in the nineteenth century lived in distinctive communities and ones that were perceived by the dominant Euro-Americans as exotic and tainted. The Chinese were visibly different from other immigrants because of their skin colour, clothing, religion and language. The many who intended to be sojourners rather than permanent immigrants made little attempt to adjust to

American values and society and preferred to live apart. As few Chinese brought their wives with them there was very little family life. Men shared accommodation, remained in their communities and spent their leisure time in such traditional institutions, as theatres, temples, gambling and opium dens and brothels. For those immigrants who did not want to return to China, the prejudice and hostility to which they were exposed pushed them back into the tightly knit and predominantly male communities for mutual support. These communities were frequently run by fraternal societies of companies known as tongs. Their full-time officials became a type of governing body for all Chinese, leastwise in California, and put together strategies to defend workers. Chinatowns, frequently located in the slum areas, were despised as dens of iniquity, dirty eyesores and rat-infested holes (Mann, 1982, pp. 61, 116–18, 176–7; Takaki, 1989, pp. 117–31).

Continued persecution and then local legislation consolidated the Chinese within their communities. They could only work in the open labour market on the sufferance of white Americans when jobs were plentiful. By the late 1860s and early 1870s, when opportunities in mining and railroad construction had shrunk, urban labourers bitterly resented the cheap Chinese workers and wanted them banned. To obtain their aims they resorted to violence and anti-coolie agitation, which ultimately led to legislation at the state and then the federal level. The final indignity was heaped on the Chinese when they were banned from entering the country under the Exclusion Act of 1882. Further violence in the 1880s encouraged many Chinese to return home. When exclusion was renewed in 1892 and extended indefinitely in 1902, the Chinese population fell (Paul, 1988, pp. 157–68; White, 1991a, pp. 340–2; Tong, 2003, pp. 45–61). Not until the late twentieth century were Chinese communities able to develop in family units.

White immigrant communities

European immigrants moving westward in the mainstream and forming rural settlements on the prairies and the plains, demonstrate some of the differences between ethnic communities, whether they are white or coloured. When European immigrants appeared in the pages of traditional western histories they were compared in general terms to white native-born Americans. They either 'filled in' settlements behind mobile native-born Americans who kept moving on to new lands or they and the native-born both struggled with the environment and merged into some composite new person, the American (Walsh, 1981, pp. 55–6, 67–8). Social science research and rural history, however, have provided ample evidence to refute these notions. Recent and not so recent findings demonstrate that European newcomers pioneered virgin land and that they retained and then adapted their cultural values while accommodating the economic and political structure of the United States (Conzen, 1990). Their specific ethnic contributions, however, have been marginalised in the New Western History. But the cultural differences between ethnic group settlements and the dominant American society have contributed much to the history of the west. These differences within white groups or alternative visions of whiteness need to be recognised in the formation of western communities alongside the differences between minorities and white society.

Certainly in the rural Midwest in the late nineteenth and early twentieth centuries it has been possible to separate the identities of native-born white Americans and newly arrived white immigrants. By 1880, over half of all those farming in Wisconsin, Minnesota and Dakota were foreign-born, primarily from Europe (Conzen, 1990, p. 304; Gjerde, 1997, p. 5) and this part of the west can demonstrate the adjustments of different ethnic communities and Yankees or Americans transplanted from older settled parts of the northeast or the Old Northwest. Drawing on a range of historical work and methodologies, Jon Gjerde analysed immigrants from northwestern Europe and found that they were able to retain their ethnic cultures while becoming solid American citizens. He argued that complementary identity can offer a means of understanding whiteness of a different colour.

Migrants from Scandinavia, Germany and Ireland hoped that the upper Midwest would be a land of material success and personal freedom. Here they aimed both to farm profitably and to maintain their cultural heritage. As participants in an economy, which was endowed with abundant natural resources and an improving technology, their hard work could pay dividends. But they were also appreciative of the lack of constraints that was available in the democratic New World. Secure in their agrarian base, they deliberately chose to establish particular ethnic communities in which they could maintain at least some of their traditional mores. They built specific ethnic islands in which one community was autonomous from another community, even when they both shared the same religion. Native-born Protestant Americans disliked these various configurations of church, language and family and tried to contain such alien ways by political means, thereby creating much ethno-cultural tension in the Midwest. It was not, however, the Yankee criticism that gradually brought change, but rather the second and third generations of ethnic or hyphenated Americans who sought fewer cultural restrictions and more opportunity to gain more equality and freedom and, in turn, to be different. The complex and multi-directional process by which individual communities were both ethno-cultural and still belonged to the larger American framework points to the varieties of whiteness that existed in the building of the American west (Gjerde, 1997).

The Midwest has offered other examples of the ways in which white immigrant cultures have coexisted with transplanted native-born Americans in newly settled rural society. Immigrant historians have focused on the transmission of cultural practices from the Old World. Increasingly they have become more accomplished in examining the European heritage, in following specific migration patterns and settlement choices and in discussing families, including choice of partner and intergenerational transfer of land and religion. There are now many more subtleties in analysing the creation of distinctive ethnic identities and the transition from immigrant settlement to ethnic community and then to the fusion with the mainstream. Historical geographers and economic historians may prefer to emphasise environmental factors, including the land itself, technology and pressures from the market systems in what has be called an Americanisation process. But such a process that discarded European practices in favour of more rapid advancement can no longer be compressed into general sentiments. Analyses of white rural communities have become more complex and need to be integrated with minority history (Ostergren, 1983; Conzen, 1990; McQuillan, 1990; Cannon, 1991). They cannot all be called Euro-American and then described as dominant, superior or triumphant.

Mormon communities

There were also white pioneers who migrated westward to set up communities apart from others. The most long lasting and largest of these separatist and often utopian communities, were the Mormons. Composed of both native-born Americans and European immigrants, they were distinguished because they were focused on a religion that did not fit the canons of Protestant or Catholic faiths. Furthermore, their communitarianism did not fit the precepts of American individualism. Mormons were thus considered peculiar. Their persecution, both before their move to Utah and following their practice of polygamy made them aliens. In this sense they can be regarded as a minority or a racial group. Mormons formed communities 'apart' from other groups as God's chosen people.

The Mormon religion emerged in 1830 in the fervour of the 'burnt-over district', in upstate New York, a region where a variety of enthusiastic and communitarian religions took hold at a time when settlers' standards of living were rising (Cross, 1950). Though the Mormons gained converts in their home district they generated controversy both there and wherever they settled. Migrating west to escape persecution, they went first to Ohio in 1831, then in large numbers to Missouri in 1838 and then to Illinois in 1839 before finally deciding to build their new Zion in the arid Salt Lake basin in 1846. Arriving there in 1847, the Mormons survived the initial period of starvation. Subsequently, through the systematic direction of their second leader Brigham Young, they built not only Salt Lake City, but in the 1850s they also created a Mormon corridor stretching through Idaho, Wyoming and Nevada.

The early success and continued growth of Mormon communities depended, however, on more than Young's organisational skills. The overland journey from the Upper Mississippi Valley to Utah reshaped the Mormons' religious faith and social practices as well as taking them to their promised land. Their early communal solidarity was consolidated by means of a theocratic polity which provided the authority necessary to manage growth in an area requiring irrigated agriculture. The new settlements were enhanced by influxes of immigrants whose journeys were financed by the Perpetual Emigrating Fund. Furthermore, the Mormons in Utah were fortunate in that the gold rush treks to California offered a commercial market for their agricultural produce, animals and services as well as providing them with needed commodities and capital. The Mormons succeeded in establishing a distinctive community in Utah through devotion, hard work and luck (Arrington, 1958, pp. 3–160; Shipps, 1985; Arrington and Bitton, 1992, pp. 3–144).

Gentiles or non-Mormons also settled in the 'Great Basin Kingdom' and as early as the 1850s their agitation stirred the federal government to consider whether Mormons were good citizens. Two main issues of concern were polygamy and theocracy, but also at issue were the Mormons' communal economic practices that were perceived to be at odds with American individualism and the competitive ethic. Though the federal government had created the territory of Utah in 1850 following the political framework used elsewhere in the west, it became concerned about the self-regulating status of the area. As governor, Brigham Young conserved the theocratic power of the Mormon Church, the practice of plural marriage was formally announced in 1852 and non-Mormon territorial officials complained about the marginal status of Gentiles. In 1857 the government decided to send in federal troops to establish its authority. Though war was avoided the tensions created by the invasion led to the reckless Mountain Meadows Massacre of a wagon train of overlanders from Arkansas and Missouri by Mormons and Native Americans. Following a compromise the federal government resumed office, but the Mormons continued to hold power and polygamy was still practised (Arrington, 1958, pp. 161–94; Arrington and Bitton, 1992, pp. 161–72)

The Mormon majority continued to experience strained relations with the Gentiles and soldiers stationed in Utah, but they managed to preserve the fundamentals of the Great Basin kingdom. As the federal government did not officially dispose of land in Utah until the completion of the transcontinental Pacific railroad in 1869 the Mormons continued with their small, allocated allotments, planned villages and communal water-rights policies. Once federal policy was activated, the church and Mormon lawyers explained how to file claims under existing legislation and then how to redistribute the land back to existing owners. Mormon lawyers also arranged matters stemming from land grants to railroads overlapping with Mormon holdings. But in subsequent years population pressure, both Mormon and Gentile, and land scarcity strained the systematic church planning of settlements. Agitation about block voting by Mormons, especially after women were given the vote in 1870, and the continued opposition to polygamy created more stresses as the Mormon oligarchy attempted to retain their traditional values. The federal government became more determined to break the political and economic power of the Mormon Church and used the flamboyant issue of polygamy to gain national support. In 1887 Congress legislated for the dismemberment of the church, confiscating its property and disfranchising women. Mormon leaders decided to abolish polygamy when threatened with disfranchisement and disbanded the People's Party, the Mormon means of controlling territorial politics. Following these changes Utah was admitted into the Union as a state. The distinctive kingdom of Mormon communities did not die, but its grip was weakened and it became easier for non-Mormons to live as Americans rather than as Gentiles in the Great Basin area (Paul, 1988, pp. 169–82; Arrington and Bitton, 1992, pp. 170–84).

Transient communities

Not all religions were as unusual as Mormonism, but there were other religious experiences in the west that fostered distinctive, albeit transient, communities prior to the development of more traditional institutional arrangements. In the early trans-Appalachian west pioneers were too widely scattered and too indigent to support permanent churches. But religious life did not stop. Local farmer-preachers and evangelisers spread the gospel and Protestant denominations, most notably the Methodists, adopted formally appointed circuit riders to ensure that their members were not left without the benefit of clergy. These circuit riders travelled from farm to farm preaching the word of God and living on the hospitality of their congregants. They adapted the size of their circuits or mobile communities to the newly settling areas. Some operated a four- to six-week circuit covering some 300–400 miles and many early circuits had more than thirty preaching stations, though the average was some fifteen to twenty-five. These itinerant ministers not only worked in the New West of the revolutionary era, but they also moved westward with the mainstream of population serving communities in need of spiritual sustenance. Their post-Civil War circuits in Kansas and Nebraska might not be as large as they were in Kentucky, Tennessee or the Old Northwest but ministers still operated out of their saddlebags and depended on the generosity of their parishioners to provide them with hospitality and some small finance. They generally worked some seven years on the circuit in Nebraska before having a large enough community to build and support a church (Dick, 1937, pp. 332–8; Rohrbough, 1978, pp. 60–1, 146–7; Hine and Faragher, 2000, pp. 365–7).

Circuit riders were not the only adaptations that organised religion made to tap into the new large parish otherwise known as the west. Camp meetings, held in the late summer, were more transient communities. These offered flexible gatherings for early settlers who travelled from a radius of forty to fifty miles to gain spiritual welfare. Open-air meetings were already known in Europe, but the versions developed in the American west were more prolonged and frequently intense. Given the abundance of geographical space it was possible to hold large gatherings in the midst of nature. Here attendees could believe that communications with God were simpler and more direct. Early pioneers often camped out for several days, listening to different preachers extolling the virtues of salvation or the damnations of hell-fire.

Camp meetings were extremely emotional assemblies or meetings, in which conversion experiences were common. They were also major social gatherings for isolated pioneers enabling both women and men to exchange information, gossip and enjoy pastimes. At the same time an unruly element, such as charlatans, drinks' pedlars, thieves and vagrants threatened theft and petty crime. Highly visible in the Kentucky and Tennessee regions in the 1790s and 1800s, they were also part of the early religious experiences in the Old Northwest in the 1820s and 1830s and moved across the Mississippi and Missouri Rivers after the Civil War. Though these later meetings were often weekend affairs, they still provided a needed focus for religious observance in those areas of the west where there were too few ministers or inadequate finance to establish a church (Moats, 1928; Dick, 1937, pp. 341–7; Sweet, W. W. 1946, pp. 44–50, 55, 56, 68–9, 440, 552, 720–1; Faragher, 1986, pp. 162–4). Religion, even in its transient format, was a strong medium for creating bonds and networks among the highly mobile population of the American west.

If itinerant ministers and camp meetings were transient forms of religious communities, the overland wagon trains were transient forms of secular communities. Groups of families and single persons, most frequently men, travelled to the Pacific coast in the 1830–50s along the great migration roads, the Oregon and California Trails. They stayed together for some five to six months, some reluctantly, others pleased to have company and some security. Some migrants knew each other before they gathered to join wagon parties; others were initially strangers. They all shared an experience that was character forming. The 'overlanders' departed from such Missouri River towns as St. Joseph, Leavenworth and Independence, travelling along the valley of the Platte River, to South Pass in the Rockies and then to Fort Hall where they split. The Oregonians followed the difficult path of the Snake River and climbed the steep slopes of the Blue Mountains, before ferrying or canoeing themselves down the Columbia River. The Californians moved south across Nevada and then through the vicious heat of the Humboldt Desert only to face the steep slopes of the Sierra Mountains before reaching the Sacramento Valley (Unruh, 1979).

This was not a journey for the faint-hearted. It was lengthy and slow, and it was also difficult, demanding and full of natural hazards. Some 10,000 migrants lost their lives on the overland trails (White, 1991a, p. 199). The major hazard was disease, particularly cholera, rather than accidents or attacks by native peoples. Other important problems were maintaining morale in the face of adverse conditions, keeping peace within the wagon train and between the migrants and the native peoples, avoiding delays and following a proven route. There were always hardships and unexpected difficulties, but some of the notorious trail disasters, like that of the Donner party of 1846–7, caught by delays and factional discord in the early snows of the Sierra Mountains, were early tragedies that were subsequently avoided (White, 1991a, pp. 204–7).

Women were important to trail welfare. At times they were weavers of community togetherness, if not solidarity, as they struggled to preserve the integrity of family life and networked with their female companions about their changed domestic tasks. At other times men were in charge as they decided the route of the journey, the length of the daily travel and whether to lighten the loads and to hunt for food. Their decisions were not always popular and were often authoritarian, leading to some splitting up of groups. However, in a society that was patriarchal, they aimed to maintain the integrity of their transient community by their traditional male power as well as by other means like rational argument and practical experience (Unruh, 1979, pp. 118–301; Schlissel, 1992; Jeffrey, 1998, pp. 35–64).

In understanding the experiences of the 'overlanders', women and men perceived the journey from different gendered perspectives. Their numerous diaries and accounts reveal tensions, but also opportunities. Historians, using these primary sources, have debated whether life in the trail communities facilitated changes in sex roles. Women found it was possible to undertake male roles of driving wagons, loading and unloading, pitching tents and taking care of the stock as well as their own domestic duties in transient circumstances. These tasks left them exhausted, as they faced major adjustments in cooking, washing, childcare and nursing and taking on any other responsibilities. But these challenges left them mentally stronger and more flexible in facing the difficulties of settling in new areas. For the one in five women who were at some stage of pregnancy on the journey, their lives were more complicated, but they too adjusted, whether out of necessity or enjoying new tasks (Schlissel, 1992; Jeffrey, 1998, pp. 35–64). For men, looking after the animals and driving the wagon were the two main occupations, but in the absence of regular farm work they also repaired wagons and tools, hunted, stood guard at night and took on any defensive role (Faragher, 1979). There is also some evidence that when necessity required they helped with some domestic tasks like washing and cooking. Indeed, on many of the journeys to the California gold mines, male-dominant groups were obliged to become domesticated. Though traditional gender roles may have been preferred, there is no doubt that arrangements shifted and women took on more responsibilities, even full responsibilities, when they were widowed. Men were also able to adapt, but seemed more reluctant to take on feminine roles, albeit temporarily. Transient communities were interesting parts of western social life in which considerable adjustments were needed. Their existence and nature continues to be part of the search for establishing western diversity.

Urban communities

Western communities were urban as well as rural. Early ventures in co-operation or belonging to a group of like-minded individuals often took the form of working towards establishing institutions that were regarded as mainstays of villages or towns, for example a school, a church, a county with officials and perhaps a post office. Others were organised for leisure purposes and for educational enhancement. Such endeavours could promote a sense of solidarity and boost town well-being. They were essential to urban life. But as villages and towns grew into cities, many more communities developed. These could then be divisive instruments, highlighting tensions and differences between gender, class and ethno-racial groups.

Clubs or voluntary associations often united respectable women who wanted to change, or from their perspective, improve early styles of western life and work. As moral reformers, women's associations attacked gambling, alcohol, prostitution and drugs. Gender differences among historians as well as among communities at the time have stimulated debate about the role and impact of such upright western women. Traditionally historians perceived that early western towns, built round mineral and lumber exploitation and cattle-driving, were male dominant in their demography and were susceptible to becoming dens of iniquity. In the absence of wives and families males behaved badly indulging in a range of vices in their leisure time. They drank, gambled, fought, patronised dance halls and bought sex because they lacked the civilising influence of 'good' women. Such escapades were part of the adventure of the American west. Women's historians, however, often viewed the seedy districts as sites of opportunity to demonstrate the need for social housekeeping. According to the ideology of the cult of domesticity women held the moral high ground and men lacked virtue and became rash, irresponsible and lustful when on their own. Mining or cattle towns needed the womanly touch to become socially acceptable.

More recent research has demonstrated that though there were many female reforming groups in western towns, women's groups were not alone in pursuing moral change. Like-minded men were also involved in cleaning up their towns. As white-collar professionals and merchants they needed to build the reputation of their society for stability and to show outsiders that they shared the tenets of the Victorian codes of conduct of respectability and the gospel of wealth. Together these female and male reformers were part of the community of honourable people who wished to influence the standards of local economic and social life. They sometimes succeeded in restricting the explicit presence of saloons and brothels, which were a central part of early western urban life, but they rarely eliminated these sites of disorder. What is at issue here, however, is not so much their success, but that women, educated in Victorian cultural standards got together to pursue moral reform. When they found that they needed political power to support their campaigns they aligned themselves with compatible men. Their reforming communities were part of the process by which western urban societies matured (Riley, 1988, pp. 147–93; Haywood, 1991; Jeffrey, 1998, pp. 162–71, 214–37).

When middle-class women attempted to convert the west to their standards of morality, they were also attacking the livelihood of another female community, that of working-class prostitutes. These women had migrated west in search of economic opportunity. Their work was hazardous and brutal. Threatened by physical violence, venereal disease, legal prosecution and social ostracism, only a few women earned a good living. Some gained a competence, but many 'scraped by' or became destitute. There was a considerable difference between the prostitutes who became property-owning capitalists in Helena, Montana, and the workers who lived in cribs on the margins of mining districts. The Chinese prostitutes, who were virtually slaves, had much less freedom than had the white sex workers on the Comstock Lode, Nevada. Nevertheless, from the perspective of the reforming women, they were all inferior, 'bad' women who corrupted society rather than workers who saw an opportunity to earn a living through providing needed services in male-dominant communities. Only their commercial importance to some sectors of the business community and the blind eye of the law enabled prostitutes to survive as a community of workers (Goldman, 1981; Butler, 1985; Petrik, 1987, pp. 25–58; Haywood, 1991, pp. 27–32).

Prostitutes were not the only group of western workers to struggle to survive among poor working conditions and hostile attitudes.

Many unskilled and semi-skilled labourers were similarly disadvantaged. Padrones and corporate managers exploited immigrant migrant workers who picked fruit and vegetables, built railroads and worked on the tracks (Peck, 2000). Both they and their native-born counterparts in mining and lumbering worked for meagre wages in dangerous conditions which were life- and limb-threatening. Though many of these workers were transitory, they developed a camaraderie that grew out of shared exploitative experiences.

Miners possibly faced the worst circumstances. In the hard-rock metal mines, explosions, cave-ins, fires and accidents involving machinery crippled or killed them. Other adverse workplace conditions included heat, impure air, dampness and scalding water. Very high temperatures in deep mines could cause death, and the contrast between these and the sub-freezing temperatures above ground could lead to pneumonia. Poor ventilation encouraged accumulations of carbon monoxide causing headaches and dizziness while quartz dust, silver and lead compounds and unburned nitro-glycerine triggered silicosis and phthisis (Wyman, 1979, pp. 84–117; Murphy, M. 1997, pp. 16–9; Jameson, 1998, pp. 90–1). Mechanisation only served to increase dangers. The annual fatality rate in western hard-rock mines in the late 1870s was one in every eighty men; the disability rate was one in every thirty men (White, 1991a, p. 281). There were major health and safety issues in the hard-rock mining industry.

Western coal-miners were little, if any, safer than their hard-rock counterparts. Colorado, as the eighth largest coal-producing state in the nation at the turn of the twentieth century, supplying fuel for the railroads and western industry, witnessed major fatal catastrophes. The explosion at Crested Butte mine in January 1884 destroyed 59 lives. Those at the Primero mine cost 24 lives in 1907 and between 75 and 150 in 1910. The explosion at the Colorado Fuel and Iron Company's Starkville mine in 1910 resulted in 56 deaths, while that at the Victor American Company's Number 3 mine at Delagua in the same year killed 79 miners. The death rate in the Colorado coalmines in 1910 was one per 46 miners (Long, 1989, pp. 170, 192–3, 245–7, 258–9). Such figures say nothing about serious accidents. When miners daily risked their lives, health and safety, it is not surprising that they developed a community spirit of shared experience, often marked by hostility to employers.

At first sight loggers appeared to have a safer workplace, if only because they were working outside rather than in the bowels of the earth. But they too, faced daily death and injury. The list of ever-present hazards was long. In the Lakes states in the late nineteenth century, the use of axes and saws led to severed limbs, while logs and trees crushed limbs and men both in the camps and while driving the logs downriver to the sawmills and markets. These sawmills were yet another dangerous workplace. In the Pacific Northwest of Oregon, Washington and British Columbia in the late nineteenth and early twentieth centuries, lumber production accelerated as more sophisticated tools and machinery, the use of steam power and better organisation 'industrialised the woodlands' (Robbins, 1997, pp. 205–37). But personal safety conditions did not improve. Steam power accelerated both the pace of work and the pace of accidents while the development of the high-lead system of hauling logs in the air with a cable suspended from a topped-off tree, further increased the accident rate. Furthermore, living conditions in the lumber camps were crude and unsanitary. Though not as lethal as logging, lumber mill labour was also precarious because of moving machinery and sharp saw blades, falling logs and accidents into boom ponds (Fries, 1951; Robbins, 1988, pp. 40–67; Williams, 1989, pp. 193–237, 289–330; Hak, 2000, pp. 116–67).

Many of these workers, particularly in the Mountain West and Far West, moved beyond camaraderie to formalise their discontent by joining a union when the opportunity arose. Poor wages also contributed to the formation of 'radical' organisations. Placed in a broader context, William Robbins considered that the industrial unionism which was attractive to miners and loggers in the late nineteenth and early twentieth centuries, stemmed from the highly volatile colonial-style economy of the west. Faced by hostile employers, whose sole aim was profitability, workers bonded together in a community of resistance to exploitation (Robbins, 1994, pp. 61–142). Richard Brown also sees this 'brotherhood' as an opposition to the developing corporate mindset in which unskilled labour was expendable. Brown calls this general phenom-enon the 'Western Civil War of Incorporation' and the wageworkers of the mines, mills and logging camps who resisted industrialists with strikes had counterparts among cowboys, vigilantes, farm workers, gunfighters, Native Americans and Mexicans (Brown,

1991, pp. 44–5, 87–127, 1992, pp. 74–89). Carlos Schwantes has used more traditional terminology to discuss wageworkers' communities as a precarious combination of the deep stresses of industrial capitalism with the confrontational frontier psychology of the west (Schwantes, 1987).

These wageworkers' communities took formal shape as unions and as strikers. Unions were more visible in mining, possibly on account of the longer tradition of sub-surface camaraderie and the dreadful working conditions. The unions were able to bridge divisions that had been visible among ethnic groups in earlier mining towns and they forged a working-class identity. Such a consciousness may well have been tenuous, partial and temporary, but it was sufficiently active to make its mark on western individualism. The Western Federation of Miners (WFM) founded in Butte, Montana, in 1893 expanded to become an association of some 200 locals by the end of the decade. These locals provided financial, organisational and emotional help to each other in their fight against corporate power and against capitalism. Their efforts met with mixed results. Strike action often ended in defeat, as at Cripple Creek in 1903. Employers called in government troops or hired private armies. But the unions also enjoyed some successes. By 1910 there was an eight-hour day and some protective legislation dealing with working conditions. Furthermore, mutualism in the form of aid to the sick, injured, widowed and orphans and assistance to bury the dead created more community bonds. The presence of an active class-conscious union forged a sense of solidarity among white male miners. They might not be well off or secure and they faced many bitter struggles, but they were shaping a place where masculine work was valued and workers were dignified (Wyman, 1979, pp. 149–225; Long, 1989, pp. 203–4; White, 1991a, pp. 290–3; Jameson, 1998; Renshaw, 1999, pp. 21–41).

The close connections of the WFM with the founding of the socialist and syndicalist union the Industrial Workers of the World (IWW) in 1905, hints both at the frustrations of the hard-rock miners in failing to establish the values of a working-class community by themselves and their continued faith in such a community. When the WFM withdrew from the IWW in 1906 because of factionalism and because it was too radical and visionary, both unions continued to search for arrangements that would protect workers. The WFM re-established ties with the craft union, the American Federation of Labor, (AFL) in 1911, but kept the principles of industrial unionism. The IWW appealed to the migratory wageworkers of the western extractive economy, who worked long hours in terrible conditions for low pay and suffered from periodic stretches of unemployment. They recognised that only through radical policies would they ever be able to fight the oppressive forces of corporate power. They would not succeed, but their attempts provided, however briefly, a community of interest that challenged the values of the short-term western wealth-makers (Wyman, 1979, pp. 226–55; Schwantes, 1994, pp. 443–5; Renshaw, 1999, pp. 43–95).

Epilogue

A selection of western communities from the vast range of historical possibilities points to the ways in which the narratives of the American west have become diverse in the past quarter of a century. When *The American Frontier Revisited* was published in 1981 (Walsh, 1981), it was relatively straightforward to survey the findings and discuss the debates about the history and impact of the American west. Then the field was still dominated by the Turnerian approach, whether in its traditional format as expressed by the Old Western Historians or in its revised format as tested by behavioural scientists. Since the advent of the New Western Historians and the arrival of the post-revisionists, the west has fragmented into a kaleidoscope of shapes and colours. There is no longer a dominant framework or even major frameworks; nor is there any desire to have an overarching organising thesis. Diversity is not only acceptable; it is desirable because it is inclusive rather than exclusive.

The American West: Visions and Revisions reflects many of the recent trends in cultural and demographic diversity, environmental awareness, the ranking of regional over national considerations and the flexibility of chronological borders. But it has not discarded the traditional concepts of frontier, conquest and process. Some of Turner's ideas continue to have value, if used in the open-ended way that he intended. They can still raise questions about the past of the American west, as for example, the dominant westward movement and linkages between the centre and periphery. Certainly Turner was a product of his own historical and geographical environment and some of his suggestions were blind to trends that were critical in shaping the character, development and impact of the west as, for example, aridity and demographic differences. But there has been too much emphasis on completely overturning a dated canon rather than accepting that for its time, it displayed some remarkable insights.

Historians regularly revise each other in the light of new sources and new ways of thinking. The latter often reflect the socio-political milieu of the times as well as technological and intellectual skills. The explosion of research and writing in American western history during the past quarter century has been very exciting and challenging. It has reinvigorated an historical area which had become academically unfashionable though it retained considerable popular interest. There has been much to admire as well as some to regret. To capture all the nuances of recent writing is impossible. The themes and ideas put forward in *The American West: Visions and Revisions* offer broad perspectives that draw on a range of general texts and thematic monographs.

References

Abbott, C. (1981). *Boosters and Businessmen: Popular Economic Thought and Urban Growth in the Antebellum Middle West*. Westport, CT, Greenwood Press.

Adelman, J. and Aron, S. (1999). 'From Borderlands to Borders: Empires, Nation-States and the Peoples in Between in North American History', *American Historical Review*, 104: June, 815–41.

Albers, P. (2002). 'Labor and Exchange in American Indian Society' in Deloria and Salisbury (eds.), pp. 269–86.

Albers, P. and Medicine, B. (eds.), (1983). *The Hidden Half. Studies of Plains Indian Women*. Lanham, MD, University Press of America.

Aron, S. (1994). 'Lessons in Conquest: Towards a Greater Western History', *Pacific Historical Review*, 63: May, 125–47.

Arrington, L. J. (1958). *Great Basin Kingdom. Economic History of the Latter-Day Saints, 1830–1900*. Cambridge, MA, Harvard University Press.

Arrington, L. J. and Bitton D. (1992) (2nd edn). *The Mormon Experience. A History of the Latter-day Saints*. Urbana, University of Illinois Press.

Atack, J. and Bateman, F. (1987). *To Their Own Soil. Agriculture in the Antebellum North*. Ames, Iowa State University Press.

Atack, J., Bateman F. and Parker, W. N. (2000). 'The Farm, The Farmer and the Market' in Engerman and Gallman (eds.), pp. 245–84.

Atherton, L. E. (1939). *The Frontier Merchant in Mid-America*. Columbia, University of Missouri Press.

Axtell, J. (1997). 'The Ethnohistory of Native America', in Fixico (ed.)., pp. 11–28.

Barman, J. (1991). *The West Beyond the West. A History of British Columbia*. University of Toronto Press.

Barron, H. S. (1993), 'Old Wine in New Bottles? The Perspective of Rural History', in Cartensen *et al.*, pp. 48–66.

Billington, M. and Hardaway, R. D. (eds.) (1998). *African Americans on the Racial Frontier*. Niwat, University Press of Colorado.

Billington, R. A. (1949). *Westward Expansion. A History of the American Frontier.* New York, Macmillan. (2nd edn. 1960; 3rd edn. 1967; 4th edn. 1974; 5th edn. 1982; 6th edn. abridged, Albuquerque, University of New Mexico Press, 2001).

  (1956). *The Far Western Frontier, 1830–1860.* New York, Harper & Row Publishers Inc.

  (1973). *Frederick Jackson Turner. Historian, Scholar, Teacher.* New York, Oxford University Press.

Binnema, T. (2001). *Common and Contested Ground: A Human and Environmental History of the Northwest Plains.* Norman, University of Oklahoma Press.

Binnema, T., Ens, G. J. and Macleod, R. C. (eds.) (2001). *From Rupert's Land to Canada. Essays in Honor of John E. Foster.* Edmonton, University of Alberta Press.

Boag, P. G. (1992). *Environment and Experience. Settlement Culture in Nineteenth-Century Oregon.* Berkeley, University of California Press.

Bogue, A. G. (1980). 'Land Policies and Sales' in Porter (ed.), vol. II, pp. 588–600.

  (1994). 'An Agricultural Empire' in Milner *et al.* (eds.), pp. 275–313.

  (1998). *Frederick Jackson Turner. Strange Roads Going Down.* Norman, University of Oklahoma Press.

Bolton, H. E. (1921). *The Spanish Borderlands: A Chronicle of Old Florida and the Southwest,* reprint. Albuquerque, University of New Mexico Press, 1996.

Brown, J. and Schenck, T. (2002) 'Métis, Mestizo and Mixed Blood' in Deloria and Salisbury (eds.), pp. 321–38.

Brown, J. S. H. (1980). *Strangers in Blood: Fur Company Family Marriages in Indian Country.* Vancouver, University of British Columbia Press.

Brown, R. M. (1991). *No Duty to Retreat. Violence and Values in American History and Society.* Norman, University of Oklahoma Press.

  (1992). 'Law and Order on the American Frontier: The Western Civil War of Incorporation' in McLaren, Foster and Orloff (eds.), pp. 74–89.

Bryant, K. L. Jr. (1994). 'Entering the Global Economy', in Milner *et al.* (eds.), pp. 194–235.

Butler, A. M. (1985). *Daughters of Joy, Sisters of Misery. Prostitution in the American West, 1865–1890.* Urbana, University of Illinois Press.

Calloway, C. G. (ed.) (1988). *New Directions in Indian American Policy.* Norman, University of Oklahoma Press.

Cannon, B. Q. (1991). 'Immigrants in American Agriculture', *Agricultural History,* 65:1, 17–35.

Carlson, P. H. (1998). *The Plains Indians.* College Station, Texas A & M University Press.

Carstensen, F. V., Rothstein, M. and Swanson J. A. (eds.) (1993). *Outstanding in His Field. Perspectives on American Agriculture in Honor of Wayne D. Rasmussen.* Ames, Iowa State University Press.

Cayton, A. R. L and Onuf, P. S. (1990). *The Midwest and the Nation. Rethinking the History of an American Region.* Bloomington, Indiana University Press.

Cayton, A. R. L. and Tuete, F. L. (eds.) (1998). *Contact Points. American Frontiers from the Mohawk Valley to the Mississippi, 1750–1830,* Chapel Hill, University of North Carolina Press.

Cayton, A. R. L. and Gray, S. E. (eds.) (2001). *The American Midwest. Essays on Regional History.* Bloomington, Indiana University Press.

Clark, C. (1979). 'The Household Economy, Market Exchange and the Rise of Capitalism in the Connecticut Valley, 1800–1860', *Journal of Social History,* 13:2, 169–89.

(1991). 'Economics and Culture: Opening Up the Rural History of the Early American Northeast', *American Quarterly,* 43: 2, 279–301.

Coates, P. (1994). 'Chances with Wolves: Renaturing Western History', *Journal of American Studies* 28: 2, 241–54.

Conzen, K. N. (1976). *Immigrant Milwaukee, 1836–60. Accommodation and Community in a Frontier City.* Cambridge, MA, Harvard University Press.

(1980). 'Germans' in Thernstrom *et al.* (eds.), pp. 405–25.

(1985). 'Peasant Pioneers: Generational Succession among German Farmers in Frontier Minnesota' in Hahn and Prude (eds.), pp. 168–209.

(1990). 'Immigrants in Nineteenth-Century Agricultural History' in Ferlenger (ed.), pp. 303–42.

(1994). 'A Saga of Families' in Milner *et al.* (eds.), pp. 315–57.

Cordell, L. S. and Smith, B. D. (1996). 'Indigenous Farmers' in Trigger and Washburn (eds.), Part 1, pp. 201–66.

Cornford, D. (1999). '"We All Live More Like Brutes Than Human Beings": Labor and Capital in the Gold Rush' in Rawls and Orsi (eds.), pp. 78–104.

Craig, L. A. (1993). *To Sow One Acre More. Childbearing and Farm Productivity in the Antebellum North.* Baltimore, John Hopkins University Press.

Cronon, W. (1987), 'Revisiting the Vanishing Frontier: The Legacy of Frederick Jackson Turner', *Western Historical Quarterly,* 18:2, 157–76.

(1991). *Nature's Metropolis: Chicago and the Great West.* New York, W. W. Norton.

(1992). 'Kennecott Journey: The Paths out of Town', in Cronon *et al.* (eds.), pp. 28–51.

(1994). 'Landscapes of Abundance and Scarcity' in Milner *et al.* (eds.) pp. 602–37.

Cronon, W., Miles, G. and Gitlin, J. (eds) (1992). *Under an Open Sky: Rethinking America's Western Past.* New York, W. W. Norton.

Cross, W. R. (1950). *The Burnt-over District. The Social and Intellectual History of Enthusiastic Religion in Western New York, 1800–1850*. Ithaca, Cornell University Press.

Curti, M. *et al.* (eds.) (1959). *The Making of an American Community. A Case Study of A Democracy in a Frontier County*. Stanford University Press.

Danbom, D. B. (1995). *Born in the Country. A History of Rural America*. Baltimore, Johns Hopkins University Press.

Danhof, C. H. (1969). *Change in Agriculture. The Northern United States, 1820–1970*. Cambridge, MA, Harvard University Press.

Dasmann, R. F. (1999). Environmental Changes before and after the Gold Rush' in Rawls and Orsi (eds.), pp. 105–22.

Davis, J. E. (1998). *Frontier Illinois*. Bloomington, Indiana University Press.

Debo, Angie (1970). *A History of the Indians of the United States*. Norman, University of Oklahoma Press.

De Leon, A. (2002). *Racial Frontiers. Africans, Chinese and Mexicans in Western America, 1848–1890*. Albuquerque, University of New Mexico Press.

Deloria, P. J. (2002). 'Historiography' in Deloria and Salisbury (eds.), pp. 6–24.

Deloria, P. J. and Salisbury, N. (eds.) (2002). *A Companion to American Indian History*. Oxford, Blackwell.

Denevan, W. M. (1992). 'The Pristine Myth: The Landscape of the Americas in 1492', *Annals of the Association of American Geographers*, 82: 3, 369–85.

Dennis, M. (1993). *Cultivating a Landscape of Peace. Iroquois-European Encounters in Seventeenth-Century America*. Ithaca, Cornell University Press.

Dick, E. [1937] (1979). *The Sod-House Frontier, 1854–1890. A Social History of the Northern Plains from the Creation of Kansas & Nebraska to the Admission of the Dakotas*. Lincoln, University of Nebraska Press.

Doti, L. P. and Schweikart, L. (1991). *Banking in the American West: From Gold Rush to Deregulation*. Norman, University of Oklahoma Press.

Edmunds, R. D. (1995). 'Native Americans, New Voices: American Indian History, 1895–1995', *American Historical Review*, 100: 3, 717–40.

Elkins, S. and McKitrick E. (1954). 'A Meaning for Turner's Frontier', *Political Science Quarterly*, 69: September, 321–53.

Emmons, D. M. (1994). 'Constructed Province: History and the Making of the Last American West', *Western Historical Quarterly*, 25: 4, 436–59.

(1998a). 'Irish Miners: From the Emerald Isle to Copper Butte' in Luebke (ed.), pp. 49–64.

(1998b) 'Safe and Steady Work: The Irish and the Hazards of Butte' in Luebke (ed.), pp. 91–107.

Encyclopedia of the American West (1996). Phillips C. and Axelrod A. (eds.) 4 vols. New York, Simon and Schuster Macmillan.

Engerman, S. L. and Gallman, R. E. (eds.) (2000). *The Cambridge Economic History of the United States*, vol. II: *The Long Nineteenth Century*. Cambridge University Press.

Etulain, R. W. (1999). *Telling Western Stories. From Buffalo Bill to Larry McMurty*. Albuquerue, University of New Mexico Press.

Etulain, R. W. (ed.) (1991). *Essays on Major Western Historians*. Albuquerque, University of New Mexico Press.

Faragher, J. M. (1979). *Women and Men on the Overland Trail*. New Haven, Yale University Press.

(1986). *Sugar Creek. Life on the Illinois Prairie*. New Haven, Yale University Press.

Ferlenger, L. (ed.) (1990). *Agriculture and National Development. Views on the Nineteenth Century*. Ames, Iowa State University Press.

Fiege, M. (1999). *Irrigated Eden. The Making of an Agricultural Landscape in the American West*. Seattle, University of Washington Press.

Fisher, R. (1996).'The Northwest from the Beginning of Trade with the Europeans to the 1880s' in Trigger and Washburn (eds.), Part 2, pp. 117–82.

Fite, G. C. (1966). *The Farmers' Frontier, 1865–1900*. New York, Holt, Rinehart and Winston.

Fixico, D. L. (1997a). 'Methodologies in Reconstructing Native American History' in Fixico (ed.), pp. 117–30.

(ed.) (1997b). *Rethinking American Indian History*. Albuquerque, University of New Mexico Press.

Flores, D. (1991).'Bison Ecology and Bison Diplomacy Redux', *Journal of American History*, 78: September, 465–85.

(2001).*The Natural West. Environmental History in the Great Plains and the Rocky Mountains*. Norman, University of Oklahoma Press.

Frankenberg, R. (1997a). 'Introduction: Local Whiteness, Localizing Whiteness' in Frankenberg (ed.), pp. 1–33.

(ed.) (1997b). *Displacing Whiteness. Essays in Social and Cultural Criticism*. Durham, Duke University Press.

Fries, R. F. (1951). *Empire in Pine. The Story of Lumbering in Wisconsin, 1830–1900*. Madison, State Historical Society of Wisconsin.

Galbraith, J. S. (1957). *The Hudson's Bay Company as an Imperial Factor*. Berkeley, University of California Press.

Gardner, J. B. and Adams, G. R. (eds.) (1983). *Ordinary People and Everyday Life. Perspectives on the New Social History*. Nashville, TN, American Association of State and Local History.

Gates, P. W. (1968). *History of Public Land Law Development*. Washington, DC, US Government Printing Office.

Gibson, A. M. (1980). *The American Indian. Prehistory to the Present*. Lexington, D. C. Heath and Company.

Gibson, J. R. (1976). *Imperial Russia in Frontier America*. New York, Oxford University Press.

(1985). *Farming the Frontier. The Agricultural Opening of the Oregon Country, 1786–1846*. Vancouver, University of British Columbia Press.

Gitlin, J. (1994). 'Empires of Trade, Hinterlands of Settlement', in Milner *et al.* (eds.), pp. 79–113.

Gjerde, J. (1991). ' "Roots of Maladjustment" in the Land: Paul Wallace Gates', *Reviews in American History*, 19: 1, 142–53.

(1997). *The Minds of the West. Ethnocultural Evolution in the Rural Middle West, 1830–1917*. Chapel Hill, University of North Carolina Press.

Goetzmann, W. H. and Goetzmann, W. N. (1986). *The West of the Imagination*. New York, W. W. Norton.

Goldman, M. (1981). *Gold Miners and Silver Diggers. Prostitution and Social Life on the Comstock Lode*. Ann Arbor, University of Michigan Press.

Gressley, G. M. (1966). *Bankers and Cattlemen*. Lincoln, University of Nebraska Press.

(ed.) (1994). *Old West/New West: Quo Vadis*. Worland, WY, High Plains Publishing Company.

Gutiérrez, R. A. (1991). *When Jesus Christ Came, the Corn Mothers Went Away. Marriage, Sexuality and Power in New Mexico, 1500–1846*. Stanford University Press.

Haeger, J. D. (1986). 'Economic Development of the American West' in Nichols (ed.), pp. 27–50.

Hagan, W. T. (1997). 'The New Indian History' in Fixico (ed.), pp. 29–42.

Hahn, S. and Prude, J. (eds.) (1985). *The Countryside in the Age of Capitalist Transformation*. Chapel Hill, University of North Carolina Press.

Haines, M. R. (2000). 'The Population of the United States, 1790–1920' in Engerman and Gallman (eds.), pp. 143–205.

Hak, G. (2000). *Turning Trees into Dollars. The British Columbia Coastal Lumber Industry, 1858–1913*. University of Toronto Press.

Hämäläinen, P. (2001). 'The First Phase of Destruction. Killing the Southern Plains Buffalo, 1790–1840', *Great Plains Quarterly*, 21: Spring, 101–14.

Hampsten, E. (1991). *Settlers' Children: Growing Up on the Great Plains*. Norman, University of Oklahoma.

Hays, S. P. (1959). *Conservation and the Gospel of Efficiency*. Cambridge, MA, Harvard University Press.

Haywood, C. R. (1991). *Victorian West. Class and Culture in Kansas Cattle Towns*. Lawrence, University Press of Kansas.

Hennessey, C. A. M. (1978). *The Frontier in Latin American History*. London, Edward Arnold.

Henretta, J. A. (1978). 'Families and Farms: *Mentalité* in Pre-Industrial America', *William and Mary Quarterly*, 3rd ser. 35: January, 3–32.

Higham, C. L. (2000). *Noble, Wretched and Redeemable. Protestant Missionaries to the Indians in Canada and the United States, 1820–1900.* Albuquerque, University of New Mexico Press.

Hine, R. V. and Faragher, J. M. (2000). *The American West. A New Interpretive History*, New Haven, Yale University Press.

Hogan, R. (1990). *Class and Community in Frontier Colorado.* Lawrence, University Press of Kansas.

Hornbeck, D. (1976). 'Mexican-American Land-Tenure Conflict in California', *The Journal of Geography*, 74: April, 209–21.

Hounshell, D. A. (1984) *From the American System to Mass Production, 1800–1932.* Baltimore, Johns Hopkins University Press.

Hoxie, F. E. (1984). *A Final Promise. The Campaign to Assimilate the Indians, 1880–1920.* Lincoln, University of Nebraska Press.

Huntley, N. (1996).'Water and the West in Historical Imagination', *Western Historical Quarterly*, 27: Spring, 5–31.

Hurt, R. D. (1987). *Indian Agriculture in America. Prehistory to Present*, Lawrence, University Press of Kansas.

(1989). 'Historians and the Northwest Ordinance'. *Western Historical Quarterly*, 20: 3, 261–80.

(1994). *American Agriculture: A Brief History.* Ames, Iowa State University Press.

Hyde, A. (1996), 'Cultural Filters: The Significance of Perception', in Milner (ed.), pp. 175–201.

Isenberg, A. C. (2000). *The Destruction of the Bison: An Environmental History, 1750–1920.* New York, Cambridge University Press.

Iverson, P. (1992). 'Taking Care of the Earth and Sky' in Josephy (ed.), pp. 85–117.

(1994). 'Native Peoples and Native Histories' in Milner *et al.* (eds.), pp. 13–43.

Jackson, R. H. (1998a). 'Introduction' in Jackson (ed.), pp. 1–6.

Jackson, R. H. (ed.) (1998b). *New Views of Borderlands History.* Albuquerque, University of New Mexico Press.

Jacobs, W. (1973). 'The Indian and the Frontier in American History – A Need for Revision', *Western Historical Quarterly*, 7: 1, 43–56.

(1994). *On Turner's Trail. 100 Years of Western Writing.* Lawrence, University Press of Kansas.

Jacobson, M. F. (1998). *Whiteness of a Different Color. European Immigrants and the Alchemy of Race.* Cambridge, MA, Harvard University Press.

Jaimes, M. A, (ed.) (1992). *The State of Native America. Genocide, Colonization and Resistance.* Boston, South End Press.

Jameson, E. (1998). *All That Glitters. Class, Conflict, and Community in Cripple Creek.* Urbana, University of Illinois Press.

Jameson, E. and Armitage, S. (eds.) (1997). *Writing the Range. Race, Class and Culture in the Women's West.* Norman, University of Oklahoma Press.

Jeffrey, J. R. (1998) (rev. edn.). *Frontier Women. "Civilizing" the West? 1840–1880*. New York, Hill and Wang.

Jennings, F. (1993). *The Founders of America*. New York, W. W. Norton.

Jordan, T. G. (1993). *North American Cattle-Ranching Frontier. Origins, Diffusion and Differentiation*. Albuquerque, University of New Mexico Press.

Josephy, A. M. Jr. (ed.) (1992). *America in 1492. The World of the Indian Peoples Before the Arrival of Columbus*. New York, Alfred A. Knopf.

Klein, A. M. (1983). 'The Political Economy of Gender: A 19th Century Plains Indian Case Study' in Albers and Medicine (eds.), pp. 143–73.

Klein, K. L. (1996). 'Reclaiming the "F" Word, or Being and Becoming Postwestern', *Pacific Historical Review*, 65: May, 179–215.

Krech, S. III (1999). *The Ecological Indian. Myth and History*. New York, W. W. Norton .

Kulikoff, A. (1992). *The Agrarian Origins of American Capitalism*. Charlottesville, University of Virginia Press.

LaDow, B. (2000). *The Medicine Line. Life and Death on a North American Borderland*. NewYork, Routledge.

Lamar, H. R. (2000) (rev. edn.). *The Far Southwest, 1846–1912. A Territorial History*. Albuquerque, University of New Mexico Press.

Lamar, H. and Thompson, L. (eds.) (1981). *The Frontier in History. North America and Southern Africa Compared*. New Haven, Yale University Press.

Lampard, E. E. (1963). *The Rise of the Dairy Industry in Wisconsin: A Study in Agricultural Change, 1820–1920*. Madison, State Historical Society of Wisconsin.

Langer, E. and Jackson, R. H. (eds) (1995). *The New Latin American Mission History*. Lincoln, University of Nebraska Press.

Lansing, M. (2000). 'Plains Indian Women and Interracial Marriage in the Upper Missouri Trade, 1804–1868', *Western Historical Quarterly*, 31: Winter, 413–33.

Le Duc, T. (1963). 'History and Appraisal of U. S. Land Policy to 1862' in Ottoson (ed.), pp. 3–27.

Levy, J. A. (1992). *They Saw the Elephant. Women and the California Gold Rush*. Norman, University of Oklahoma Press.

Limbaugh, R. H. (1999). 'Making Old Tools Work Better: Pragmatic Adaptation and Innovation in Gold-Rush Technology', in Rawls and Orsi (eds.), pp. 24–51.

Limerick, P. N. (1987). *Legacy of Conquest. The Unbroken Past of the American West*. New York, W. W. Norton.

   (1991). 'Persistent Traits and the Persistent Historian: The American Frontier and Ray Allen Billington' in Etulain (ed.), pp. 277–310.

Limerick, P. N., Milner, C. A, Rankin, C. E. (eds.) (1991). *Trails: Toward A New Western History*. Lawrence, University Press of Kansas.

Long, P. (1989). *Where the Sun Never Shines. A History of America's Bloody Coal Industry*. New York, Paragon House.

Lowie, R. H. (1954). *Indians of the Plains*. American Museum of Natural History. Reprint 1963, Garden City, Natural History Press.

Luebke, F.C. (1998a) 'Introduction' in Luebke (ed.), pp. vii–xix.

(ed.) (1998b). *European Immigrants in the American West. Community Histories*. Albuquerque, University of New Mexico Press.

Lurie, N. O. (1978). 'The Indian Claims Commission', *Annals of the American Academy of Political and Social Science*, 436, 97–110.

McLaren, J., Foster, H. and Orloff, C. (eds.) (1992). *Law for the Elephant, Law for the Beaver. Essays on the Legal History of the North American West*. Regina, Canadian Plains Research Center.

McQuillan, D. A. (1990). *Prevailing Over Time. Ethnic Adjustment on the Kansas Prairies, 1875–1925*. Lincoln, University of Nebraska Press.

Madison, J. H. (1997). 'Diverging Trails. Why the Midwest is Not the West', in Ritchie and Hutton (eds.), pp. 43–53.

Mahoney,T. R. (1990). *River Towns in the Great West. The Structure of Provincial Urbanization in the American Midwest, 1820–1870*. New York, Cambridge University Press.

Malin, J. C. (1947). *Grasslands of North America: Prolegomena to Its History*. Lawrence, KS, J. C. Malin.

Mann, R. (1982). *After the Gold Rush: Society in Grass Valley and Nevada City, California, 1849–1870*. Stanford University Press.

May, D. L. (1994). *Three Frontiers. Family, Land and Society in the American West, 1850–1900*. New York, Cambridge University Press.

Mayhew, A. (1972). 'A Reappraisal of the Causes of Farm Protest in the United States, 1870–1900', *Journal of Economic History*, 32: 2, 464–75.

Meinig, D. M. (1986). *The Shaping of America. A Geographical Perspective of 500 Years of History. Vol. 1 Atlantic America, 1492–1800*. New Haven, Yale University Press.

(1993). *The Shaping of America. A Geographical Perspective of 500 Years of History. Vol. 2 Continental America, 1800–1867*. New Haven, Yale University Press.

Mercier, L. (1997). '"We Are Women Irish": Gender, Class, Religious and Ethnic Identity in Anaconda, Montana' in Jameson and Armitage (eds.), pp. 311–33.

(2001). *Anaconda. Labor, Community and Culture in Montana's Smelter City*. Urbana. University of Illinois Press.

Merrill, M. (1977). 'Cash is Good to Eat: Self-Sufficiency and Exchange in the Rural Economy of the United States', *Radical History Review*, 3, 42–71.

Meyer, M. L. and Thornton, R. (1988). 'Indians and the Numbers Game: Quantitative Methods in Native American History' in Calloway (ed.), pp. 5–29.

Milner, C. A. (ed.) (1996). *A New Significance. Re-Envisioning the History of the American West.* New York, Oxford University Press.

Milner, C. A., O'Connor, C. A. and Sandweiss, M. A. (eds.). (1994). *The Oxford History of the American West.* New York, Oxford University Press.

Miner, C. (1986). *West of Wichita. Settling the High Plains of Kansas, 1865–1890.* Lawrence, University Press of Kansas.

Moats, F. I. (1928). 'The Rise of Methodism in the Middle West', *The Mississippi Valley Historical Review,* 15: 1 (June), 69–88.

Mokyr J. (ed.) (2003). *The Oxford Encyclopedia of Economic History.* New York, Oxford University Press.

Murphy, L. E. (2000). *A Gathering of Rivers. Indians, Métis and Mining in the Great Lakes, 1737–1832.* Lincoln, University of Nebraska Press.

Murphy, M. (1997). *Mining Cultures. Men Women and Leisure in Butte, 1914–41.* Urbana, University of Illinois Press.

Myres, S. L. (1982). *Westering Women and the Frontier Experience, 1800–1915.* Albuquerque, University of New Mexico Press.

Nash, G. D. (1994). 'The Global Contest of the New Western Historian', in Gressley (ed.), pp. 147–62.

Nash, R. [1967](1973) (rev. edn.) *Wilderness and the American Mind.* New Haven, Yale University Press.

Neth, M. (1995). *Preserving the Family Farm. Women, Community and the Foundations of Agribusiness in the Midwest, 1900–1940.* Baltimore, Johns Hopkins University Press.

Nichols, R. L. (ed.) (1986). *American Frontier and Western Issues. A Historiographical Review.* Westport, Greenwood Press.

Nichols, R. L. (1998). *Indians in the United States and Canada. A Comparative History.* Lincoln, University of Nebraska Press.

Nugent, W. (1989). 'Frontiers and Empires in the Late Nineteenth Century', *Western Historical Quarterly,* 20: 4, 394–408.

(1992). 'Where is the American West? Report on a Survey', *Montana, the Magazine of Western History,* 42: 3, 2–23.

[1999] (2001). *Into the West. The Story of Its People.* New York, Vintage Books.

O'Connor, C. A. (1994). 'A Region of Cities' in Milner *et al.* (eds.), pp. 535–63.

Oglesby, R. E. (1963). *Manuel Lisa and the Opening of the Missouri Fur Trade.* Norman, University of Oklahoma Press.

(1988). 'Ray Allen Billington', in Wunder (ed.), pp. 97–121.

Osgood, E. S. (1929). *The Day of the Cattleman.* Minneapolis, University of Minnesota Press.

Ostergren, R. C. (1983). 'European Settlement and Ethnicity Patterns on the Agricultural Frontiers of South Dakota', *South Dakota History,* 13: 1–2, pp. 49–82.

(1998). 'Prairie Bound: Migration Patterns to a Swedish Settlement on the Dakota Frontier' in Luebke (ed.), pp. 15–31.

Ottoson, H. (1963) (ed.). *Land Use Policy and Problems in the United States*, Lincoln, University of Nebraska Press.

Painter, N. I. (1971). *Exodusters: Black Migration to Kansas After Reconstruction*. New York, Knopf.

Paul, R. W. (1947). *California Gold. The Beginning of Mining in the Far West*. Cambridge, MA, Harvard University Press.

(1963). *Mining Frontiers of the Far West, 1848–1880*. New York, Holt, Rinehart and Winston.

(1988). *The Far West and the Great Plains in Transition, 1859–1900*. New York, Harper & Row.

Payne, M. (2001). 'Fur Trade Historiography. Past Conditions, Present Circumstances and a Hint of Future Prospects' in Binnema *et al.* (eds.), pp. 3–22.

Peck, G. (2000). *Reinventing Free Labor. Padrones and Immigrant Workers in the North American West, 1880–1930*. New York, Cambridge University Press.

Perkins, B. (1993). *The Creation of a Republican Empire, 1776–1865*. Cambridge University Press.

Peterson, J. and Brown, J. H. S. (eds.) (1985). *Being and Becoming Métis in North America*. Winnipeg, University of Manitoba Press.

Petrik, P. (1987). *No Step Backwards. Women and Family on the Rocky Mountain Mining Frontier, Helena, Montana, 1865–1990*. Helena, Montana Historical Society Press.

Petulla, J. M. (1988) (2nd edn.). *American Environmental History*. Columbus, OH, Merrill Pub. Co.

Pisani, D. J. (1984). *From the Family Farm to Agribusiness: The Irrigation Crusade in California and the West, 1850–1931*. Berkeley, University of California Press.

(1988). 'Deep and Troubled Waters: A New Field of Western History? *New Mexico Historical Review*, 63: October., 311–31.

(1992). *To Reclaim A Divided West. Water, Law and Public Policy, 1848–1902*. Albuquerque, University of New Mexico Press.

(1996). *Water, Land and Law in the West. The Limits of Public Policy, 1850–1920*. Lawrence, University Press of Kansas.

Pomeroy, E. (1965). *The Pacific Slope. A History of California, Oregon, Washington, Idaho, Utah and Nevada*. Seattle, University of Washington Press.

Porter, G. (ed.)(1980). *Encyclopedia of American Economic History*, 3 vols. New York, C. Scribner's Sons.

Porter, K. W. (1931). *John Jacob Astor Business Man*, 2 vols. Cambridge MA, Harvard University Press.

Potter, D. M. (1954). *People of Plenty. Economic Abundance and the American Character*. University of Chicago Press, 1954.

Prucha, F. P. (1984). *The Great Father. United States Government and the American Indians.* Lincoln, University of Nebraska Press.

Rawls, J. J. and Orsi, R. J. (eds.) (1999). *A Golden State. Mining and Economic Development in Gold-Rush California.* Berkeley, University of California Press.

Ray, A. J. [1974] (1998). *Indians in the Fur Trade* (With a New Introduction). University of Toronto Press.

(1996). *I Have Lived Here Since the World Began. An Illustrated History of Canada's Native People.* Toronto, Lester Publishing Limited.

Ray, A. J. and Freeman, D. B. (1978). *"Give Us Good Measure": An Economic Analysis of Relations Between the Indians and the Hudson's Bay Company Before 1763.* University of Toronto Press.

Renshaw, P. [1967](1999), (updated edn). *The Wobblies. The Story of the IWW and Syndicalism in the United States.* Chicago, Ivan, R. Dee.

Richter, D. K. (1992). *The Ordeal of the Longhouse. The Peoples of the Iroquois League in the Era of European Colonization.* Chapel Hill, University of North Carolina Press.

(2001). *Facing East from Indian Country. A Native History of Early America.* Cambridge, MA, Harvard University Press.

Ridge, M. (1987). 'Ray Allen Billington, Western History and American Exceptionalism', *Pacific Historical Review*, 56: November, 495–511.

Riley, G. G. (1988). *The Female Frontier. A Comparative View of Women on the Prairie and the Plains.* Lawrence, University Press of Kansas.

Ritchie, R. C. and Hutton, P. A. (eds.) (1997). *Frontier and Region. Essays in Honor of Martin Ridge.* San Marino, CA, The Huntington Library Press.

Robbins, W. G. (1985). *American Forestry. A History of National, State and Private Cooperation.* Lincoln, University of Nebraska Press.

(1988). *Hard Times in Paradise. Coos Bay, Oregon, 1850–1986.* Seattle, University of Washington Press.

(1994). *Colony and Empire: The Capitalist Transformation of the West.* Lawrence, University Press of Kansas.

(1997). *Landscapes of Promise. The Oregon Story 1800–1940.* Seattle, University of Washington Press.

(ed.) (2001). *The Great Northwest. The Search for Regional Identity.* Corvallis, Oregon State University Press.

Roediger, D. (1994a). 'Whiteness and Ethnicity in the History of White Ethnics in the US' in Roediger (ed.), pp. 181–98.

(ed.) (1994b). *Towards the Abolition of Whiteness. Essays on Race, Politics and Working Class History.* London, Verso.

Rohe, R. (1986). 'Man and the Land. Mining's Impact in the Far West', *Arizona and the West*, 28: Winter, 299–338.

(1995). 'Environment and Mining in the Mountainous West', in Wyckoff and Dilsaver (eds.), pp.169–93.

Rohrbough, M. J. (1978). *The Trans-Appalachian Frontier. Peoples, Societies and Institutions, 1775–1850*. New York, Oxford University Press, (1997). *Days of Gold. The California Gold Rush and the American Nation*. Berkeley, University of California Press.

Roundtable (1994). 'Six Responses to "Constructed Province" and a Final Statement by the Author', *Western Historical Quarterly*, 25: 4, 461–86.
(1990). 'Environmental History', *Journal of American History* 76: 4, 1087–147.
(2000). 'Claims and Prospects of Western History', *Western Historical Quarterly*, 30: Spring, 25–46.

Salisbury, N. (1996). 'Native People and European Settlers in Eastern North America, 1600–1783' in Trigger and Washburn (eds.), Part 1, pp. 399–460.

Schlissel, L. (ed.) [1982](1992) (2nd edn.) *Women's Diaries of the Westward Journey*. New York, Schocken Books.

Schwantes, C. A. (1987). 'The Concept of the Wageworkers' Frontier: A Framework for Future Research', *Western Historical Quarterly*, 18: 1, 39–55.
(1994). 'Wage Earners and Wealth Makers' in Milner, *et al.* (eds.), pp. 430–67.
[1989] (1996). *The Pacific Northwest. An Interpretive History*. Lincoln, University of Nebraska Press.

Shannon, F. A. (1945). *The Farmer's Last Frontier, 1860–1897*. New York, Holt, Rinehart and Winston.

Sharp, P. F. (1955a). 'Three Frontiers. Some Comparative Studies of Canadian, American and Australian Settlement'. *Pacific Historical Review*, 24: November, 369–77.
(1955b). *Whoop-Up Country. The Canadian-American West*. Minneapolis, University of Minnesota Press.

Shipps, J. (1985). *Mormonism. The Story of a New Religious Tradition*. Urbana, University of Illinois Press.

Skaggs, J. M. (1986). *Prime Cut: Livestock Raising and Meatpacking in the United States, 1607–1983*. College Station, Texas A & M University Press.

Sleeper-Smith, S. (2001). *Indian Women and French Men: Rethinking Cultural Encounter in the Western Great Lakes (Native Americans of the Northeast)*. Amherst, University of Massachusetts Press.

Smith, B. D. (1996). 'Agricultural Chiefdoms of the Eastern Woodlands' in Trigger and Washburn (eds.), Part 1, pp. 267–323.

Smith, D. A. [1987] (1993). *Mining America. The Industry and the Environment, 1800–1980*. Niwot, University Press of Colorado.
(1999). "This Reckless and Disastrous Practice". The Impact of Mining on Forests in the Rocky Mountains, 1859–1880', *Journal of the West*, 38: 4, 15–24.

Snow, Dean R. (1996). 'The First Americans and the Differentiation of Hunter-Gatherer Cultures' in Trigger and Washburn (eds.), Part 1, pp. 125–99.

Starr, K. and Orsi, R. J. (eds.) (2000). *Rooted in Barbarous Soil. People, Culture, and Community in Gold-Rush California*. Berkeley, University of California Press.

Statistical Atlas (1898). Eleventh Census of the United States. Washington, DC, United States Bureau of the Census.

Steckel, R. (1983). 'The Economic Foundations of East-West Migration during the Nineteenth Century', *Explorations in Economic History*, 20, 14–36.

Stiffarm, L. A. with Lane, P. Jr. (1992). 'The Demography of Native North America. A Question of American Indian Survival' in Jaimes (ed.), pp. 23–54

Stratton, J. L. (1981). *Pioneer Women. Voices from the Kansas Frontier*. New York, Simon and Schuster.

Sturtevant, W. (ed.) (2001). *Handbook of North American Indians*. Vol. XIII: parts 1 and 2, *Plains* (vol. ed. DeMallie, R. J.). Washington, Smithsonian Institution.

Sweet, D. (1995). 'The Ibero-American Frontier Mission in Native American History' in Langer and Jackson (eds.), pp. 1–48.

Sweet, W. W. (1946), *Religion on the American Frontier, 1783–1840*. Vol. IV: *The Methodists*. New York, Cooper Square Publishers Inc. (1964 reprint).

Swierenga, R. P. (1977). 'Land Speculation and its Impact on American Economic Growth and Welfare. A Historiographical Review', *Western Historical Quarterly*, 8:3, 283–302.

   (1983). 'Agriculture and Rural Life: The New Rural History' in Gardener and Adams (eds.), pp. 91–113.

   (1989). 'The Settlement of the Old Northwest: Ethnic Pluralism in a Featureless Plain', *Journal of the Early Republic*, 9: Spring, 73–105.

'Symposium on the New Western History'. (1993). Intro. Folsom, B. W. Jr, and contributions by Ridge, M., Thompson, G., Nash, G. D. and Goetzmann, W. H., *Continuity. A Journal of History*, 17: 3,1–32.

Takaki, R. (1989). *Strangers From a Different Shore. A History of Asian Americans*. New York, Penguin.

Taylor, Q. (1996). 'From Estaban to Rodney King: Five Centuries of African American History in the West', *Montana, the Magazine of Western History* 46: 4, 2–23.

   (1998). *In Search of the Racial Frontier. African Americans in the American West, 1528–1990*. New York, W. W. Norton.

Taylor Q. and Wilson Moore, S. A. (eds.) (2003). *African American Women Confront the West, 1600–2000*. Norman, University of Oklahoma Press.

Thernstorm, S. (ed.), (1980). *Harvard Encyclopedia of American Ethnic Groups.* Cambridge, MA, Belknap Press of Harvard University.

Thompson, G. (1994). 'The New Western History: A Critical Analysis' in Gressley (ed.), pp. 49–72.

Thorne, T. (1996). *The Many Hands of My Relations: French and Indians on the Lower Missouri.* Columbia, University of Missouri Press.

Thornton, R. (1987). *American Indian Holocaust and Survival. A Population History Since 1492.* Norman, University of Oklahoma Press.

(2002). 'Health, Disease and Demography' in Deloria and Salisbury (eds.), pp. 68–84.

Tong, B. [2000] (2003)(rev. edn.). *The Chinese Americans.* Boulder, University Press of Colorado.

Trigger, B. G. and Swaggerty, W. R. (1996) 'Entertaining Strangers: North America in the Sixteenth Century', in Trigger and Washburn (eds.), 325–98.

Trigger, Bruce G. and Washburn, Wilcomb E. (eds.) (1996). *The Cambridge History of the Native Peoples of the Americas*, Vol 1, Parts 1 and 2, *North America.* Cambridge University Press.

Turner, F. J. (1893). 'The Significance of the Frontier in American History'. *Annual Report* of the American Historical Association for 1893. Washington, D C, reprinted in Turner, F. J. *The Frontier in American History.* New York, Henry Holt,1920.

Utley, R. M. [1984] (2003) (rev. edn.). *The Indian Frontier of the American West.* Albuquerque, University of New Mexico Press.

Unruh, J. D. Jr. (1979). *The Plains Across. The Overland Emigrants and the Trans-Mississippi West, 1840–1860.* Urbana, University of Illinois Press.

Van Kirk, S. (1980). *Many Tender Ties. Women in Fur Trade Society, 1670–1870.* Winnipeg, Watson and Dwyer.

Waldman, C. (1985). *Atlas of the North American Indian.* New York, Facts on File Publications.

Walsh, M. (1972). *The Manufacturing Frontier. Pioneer Industry in Antebellum Wisconsin.* Madison, State Historical Society of Wisconsin.

(1981). *The American Frontier Revisited.* London, Macmillan.

(1982). *The Rise of the Midwestern Meat Packing Industry.* Lexington, The University Press of Kentucky.

(1992). 'Frederick Jackson Turner and the American Frontier', *The Historian*, 36: Winter, 3–8.

(1995). 'Women's Place on the American Frontier', *Journal of American Studies*, 29: 2, 241–55.

(1999a). 'From the Periphery to the Centre: Changing Perspectives on American Farm Women', in Walsh (ed.), 135–50.

Walsh, M. (2003). 'Meatpacking' in Mokyr (ed.), vol. III, 474–77.

Walsh, M. (ed.) (1999b). *Working Out Gender. Perspectives from Labour History.* Aldershot, Ashgate Publishing.

Warhus, M. (1997). *Another America. Native American Maps and the History of Our Land*. New York, St. Martin's Press.

Warren, L. S. (2002). 'The Nature of Conquest: Indians, Americans and Environmental History' in Deloria and Salisbury (eds.), pp. 287–306.

Webb, W. P. (1931). *The Great Plains*. New York, Ginn and Company.

(1951). *The Great Frontier*. Lincoln, University of Nebraska Press (1986 repr.).

Weber, D. J. (1992). *The Spanish Frontier in North America*. New Haven, Yale University Press.

(1994). 'The Spanish-Mexican Rim', in Milner, *et al.* (eds.), pp. 45–77.

Werner, E. E. (1995). *Pioneer Children on the Journey West*. Boulder, Westview Press.

West, E. (1989). *Growing Up with the Country: Childhood on the Far Western Frontier*. Albuquerque, University of New Mexico Press.

(1991). 'Walter Prescott Webb and the Search for the West' in Etulain (ed.), pp. 167–91.

(1995). *The Way to the West. Essays on the Central Plains*. Albuquerque, University of New Mexico Press.

(1998). *The Contested Plains. Indians, Goldseekers and the Rush to Colorado*. Lawrence, University Press of Kansas.

Whitaker, J. W. (1975). *Feedlot Empire: Beef Cattle Feeding in Illinois and Iowa, 1840–1880*. Ames, Iowa State University Press.

White, R. (1980). *Land Use, Environment and Social Change: The Shaping of Island County, Washington*. Seattle, University of Washington Press.

(1983). *The Roots of Dependency. Subsistence, Environment and Social Change among the Choctaws, Pawnees and Navajos*. Lincoln, University of Nebraska Press.

(1991a). '*It's Your Misfortune and None of Mine Own'. A New History of the American West*. Norman, University of Oklahoma Press.

(1991b). *The Middle Ground. Indians, Empires and Republics in the Great Lakes Region, 1650–1815*. New York, Cambridge University Press.

(1994). 'Animals and Enterprise' in Milner *et al.* (eds.), pp. 236–73.

(1997). 'Indian Peoples and the Natural World. Asking the Right Questions', in Fixico (ed.), pp. 87–100.

Williams, M. (1989). *Americans and Their Forests. A Historical Geography*. Cambridge University Press.

Winther, O. O. (1964). *The Transportation Frontier: Trans-Mississippi West, 1865–1890*. New York, Holt, Rinehart and Winston.

Wishart, D. J. [1979] (1992). *The Fur Trade of the American West, 1807–1840*. Lincoln, University of Nebraska Press.

(1994). *An Unspeakable Sadness. The Dispossession of the Nebraska Indians*. Lincoln, University of Nebraska Press.

Worcester, D. E. (1991). 'Herbert Eugene Bolton: The Making of a Western Historian', in Etulain (ed.), pp. 193–213.

Worster, D. (1979). *Dust Bowl. The Southern Plains in the 1930s*. New York, Oxford University Press.

(1985). *Rivers of Empire: Water, Aridity and the Growth of the American West*. New York, Pantheon Books.

(1992). *Under Western Skies. Nature and History in the American West*. New York, Oxford University Press.

(1994). *An Unsettled Country. Changing Landscapes of the American West*. Albuquerque, University of New Mexico Press.

Wrobel, D. M. (1993). *The End of American Exceptionalism. Frontier Anxiety from the Old West to the New Deal*. Lawrence, University Press of Kansas.

(1996a). 'Beyond the Frontier-Region Dichotomy', *Pacific Historical Review*, 65: August, 401–29.

(1996b) 'New Western History', in *Encyclopedia of the American West*, vol. III: pp. 1191–4.

Wrobel, D. M. and Long, P. T. (eds.) (2001). *Seeing and Being Seen. Tourism in the American West*. Lawrence, University Press of Kansas.

Wunder, J. R. (1988). *Historians of the American Frontier. A Bio-Bibliographical Source Book*. Westport, Greenwood Press.

(1994). 'What's Old about the New Western History? Race and Gender', Part 1, *Pacific Northwest Quarterly*, 85: 1, 50–8.

(1998). 'What's Old about the New Western History? Environment and Economy', *Pacific Northwest Quarterly*, 89: 2, 84–94.

Wyant, W. K. (1982). *Westward in Eden. The Public Lands and the Conservation Movement*. Berkeley, University of California Press.

Wyckoff, W. (1999). *Creating Colorado. The Making of a Western American Landscape, 1860–1940*. New Haven, Yale University Press.

Wyckoff, W. and Dilsaver, L. M. (eds.) (1995). *The Mountainous West. Explorations in Historical Geography*. Lincoln, University of Nebraska Press.

Wyman, M. (1979). *Hard Rock Epic. Western Miners and the Industrial Revolution, 1860–1910*. Berkeley, University of California Press.

Yeager, M. (1981). *Competition and Regulation. The Development of Oligopoly in the Meat Packing Industry*. Greenwich, JAI Press.

Yung, J. (1995). *Unbound Feet. A Social History of Chinese Women in San Francisco*. Berkeley, University of California Press.

Zevin, R. (1972). 'An Interpretation of American Imperialism', *Journal of Economic History*, 32: 1, 316–60.

Zhu, L. (1997). *A Chinaman's Chance. The Chinese on the Rocky Mountain Mining Frontier*. Niwot, University of Colorado Press.

Index

New Studies in Economic and Social History

Titles in the series available from Cambridge University Press:

10. J. L. Anderson
Explaining long-term economic change
ISBN 0 521 55269 9 (hardback) 0 521 55784 4 (paperback)

11. D. Baines
Emigration from Europe 1815–1930
ISBN 0 521 55270 2 (hardback) 0 521 55783 6 (paperback)

12. M. Collins
Banks and industrial finance 1800–1939
ISBN 0 521 55271 0 (hardback) 0 521 55782 8 (paperback)

13. A. Dyer
Decline and growth in English towns 1400–1640
ISBN 0 521 55272 9 (hardback) 0 521 55781 X (paperback)

14. R. B. Outhwaite
Dearth, public policy and social disturbance in England, 1550–1800
ISBN 0 521 55273 7 (hardback) 0 521 557801 (paperback)

15. M. Sanderson
Education, economic change and society in England
ISBN 0 521 55274 5 (hardback) 0 521 55779 8 (paperback)

16. R. D. Anderson
Universities and elites in Britain since 1800
ISBN 0 521 55275 3 (hardback) 0 521 55778 X (paperback)

17. C. Heywood
The development of the French economy, 1700–1914
ISBN 0 521 55276 1 (hardback) 0 521 55777 1 (paperback)

18. R. A. Houston
The population history of Britain and Ireland 1500–1750
ISBN 0 521 55277 X (hardback) 0 521 55776 3 (paperback)

19. A. J. Reid
Social classes and social relations in Britain 1850–1914
ISBN 0 521 55278 8 (hardback) 0 521 55775 5 (paperback)

20. R. Woods
The population of Britain in the nineteenth century
ISBN 0 521 55279 6 (hardback) 0 521 55774 7 (paperback)

21. T. C. Barker
The rise and rise of road transport, 1700–1990
ISBN 0 521 55280 X (hardback) 0 521 55773 9 (paperback)

22. J. Harrison
The Spanish economy
ISBN 0 521 55281 8 (hardback) 0 521 55772 0 (paperback)

23. C. Schmitz
The growth of big business in the United States and Western Europe, 1850–1939
ISBN 0 521 55282 6 (hardback) 0 521 55771 2 (paperback)

24. R. A. Church
The rise and decline of the British motor industry
ISBN 0 521 55283 4 (hardback) 0 521 55770 4 (paperback)

25. P. Horn
Children's work and welfare, 1780–1880
ISBN 0 521 55284 2 (hardback) 0 521 55769 0 (paperback)

26. R. Perren
Agriculture in depression, 1870–1940
ISBN 0 521 55285 0 (hardback) 0 521 55768 2 (paperback)

27. R. J. Overy
The Nazi economic recovery 1932–1938: second edition
ISBN 0 521 55286 9 (hardback) 0 521 55767 4 (paperback)

28. S. Cherry
Medical services and the hospitals in Britain, 1860–1939
ISBN 0 521 57126 X (hardback) 0 521 57784 5 (paperback)

29. D. Edgerton
Science, technology and the British industrial 'decline', 1870–1970
ISBN 0 521 57127 8 (hardback) 0 521 57778 0 (paperback)

30. C. A. Whatley
The Industrial Revolution in Scotland
ISBN 0 521 57228 2 (hardback) 0 521 57643 1 (paperback)

31. H. E. Meller
Towns, plans and society in modern Britain
ISBN 0 521 57227 4 (hardback) 0 521 57644 X (paperback)

32. H. Hendrick
Children, childhood and English society, 1880–1990
ISBN 0 521 57253 3 (hardback) 0 521 57624 5 (paperback)

33. N. Tranter
Sport, economy and society in Britain, 1750–1914
ISBN 0 521 57217 7 (hardback) 0 521 57655 5 (paperback)

34. R. W. Davies
Soviet economic development from Lenin to Khrushchev
ISBN 0 521 62260 3 (hardback) 0 521 62742 7 (paperback)

35. H. V. Bowen
War and British society, 1688–1815
ISBN 0 521 57226 6 (hardback) 0 521 57645 8 (paperback)

36. M. M. Smith
Debating slavery: the antebellum American south
ISBN 0 521 57158 8 (hardback) 0 521 57696 2 (paperback)

37. M. Sanderson
Education and economic decline in Britain, 1870 to the 1990s
ISBN 0 521 58170 2 (hardback) 0 521 58842 1 (paperback)

38. V. Berridge
Health policy, health and society, 1939 to the 1990s
ISBN 0 521 57230 4 (hardback) 0 521 57641 5 (paperback)

39. M. E. Mate
Women in medieval English society
ISBN 0 521 58322 5 (hardback) 0 521 58733 6 (paperback)

40. P. J. Richardson
Economic change in China c. 1800–1950
ISBN 0 521 58396 9 (hardback) 0 521 63571 3 (paperback)

41. J. E. Archer
Social unrest and popular protest in England, 1780–1840
ISBN 0 521 57216 9 (hardback) 0 521 57656 3 (paperback)

42. K. Morgan
Slavery, Atlantic trade and the British economy, 1660–1800
ISBN 0 521 58213 X (hardback) 0 521 58814 6 (paperback)

43. C. W. Chalklin
The rise of the English town, 1650–1850
ISBN 0 521 66141 2 (hardback) 0 521 66737 2 (paperback)

44. J. Cohen and G. Federico
The growth of the Italian economy, 1820–1960
ISBN 0 521 66150 1 (hardback) 0 521 66692 9 (paperback)

45. T. Balderston
Economics and politics in the Weimar Republic
ISBN 0 521 58375 6 (hardback) 0 521 77760 7 (paperback)

46. C. Wrigley
British Trade Unions since 1933
ISBN 0 521 57231 2 (hardback) 0 521 57640 7 (paperback)

47. A. Colli
The History of Family Business, 1850–2000
ISBN 0 521 80028 5 (hardback) 0 521 80472 8 (paperback)

48. D. Mühlberger
    The social Bases of Nazism, 1919–1933
    ISBN 0 521 80285 7 (hardback) 0 521 00372 5 (paperback)
49. J. P. Dormois
    The French Economy in the Twentieth Century
    ISBN 0 521 66092 0 (hardback) 0 521 66787 9 (paperback)
50. M. Walsh
    The American West. Visions and Revisions
    ISBN 0 521 593 336 (hardback) 0 521 596 718 (paperback)

Previously published as
Studies in Economic and Social History

Titles in the series available from the Macmillan Press Limited

Economic History Society

The Economic History Society, which numbers around 3,000 members, publishes the *Economic History Review* four times a year (free to members) and holds an annual conference.
Enquiries about membership should be addressed to

The Assistant Secretary
Economic History Society
PO Box 70
Kingswood
Bristol
BS15 5TB

Full-time students may join at special rates.